6-21-65

The Pastor
and the
Race Issue

The Pastor
and the
Race Issue

Daisuke Kitagawa

THE SEABURY PRESS
NEW YORK

ACKNOWLEDGMENTS

Copyrighted material has been quoted in the text from the following sources:

Dial Press, New York—James Baldwin, *Nobody Knows My Name.* Copyright © 1961 by James Baldwin. Reprinted by permission of The Dial Press.

Harper & Row, Publishers, New York—Kyle Haselden, *The Racial Problem in Christian Perspective.*

——— For the Institute for Religious Studies: F. Ernest Johnson, "What Has the War Taught the Churches?" in F. Ernest Johnson, editor, *World Order: Its Intellectual and Cultural Foundations.* Roethlisberger and Dickinson, *Management and the Worker* (Harvard University Press, 1935) quoted by Robert S. Lind, "Group and Social Status" in R. M. MacIver, editor, *Civilization and Group Relations.*

Holt, Rinehart & Winston, New York—Erich Fromm, *Man for Himself: An Inquiry into the Psychology of Ethics.*

New American Library, Signet Books, New York—John Howard Griffin, *Black Like Me.*

1311793

Preface

THIS volume is intended for the professional leadership of the Christian churches. Its express aim is to stimulate among churchmen more theologically oriented thinking on racial issues. It goes without saying that theologically oriented thinking takes seriously such disciplines as sociology, anthropology, psychology, history, and a number of others.

Some parts of this book have appeared in print before. Grateful acknowledgment is due to the Department of Racial and Cultural Relations of the National Council of Churches of Christ in the U.S.A. for the use of my article, "U.S. Race Relations in World Perspective" in the *Interracial News Service*, March-April, 1964, issue; to the World Council of Churches for the use of my two articles, "Theological and Non-Theological Factors in Race Relations" and "All in Each Place: Racial and Ethnic Factors," in the *Ecumenical Review*, April, 1961, and October, 1962, respectively. The bulk of Parts II, III, and IV was delivered as a series of lectures before Minnesota State Pastors' Conference, in Minneapolis, January, 1964.

Contents

The Pastor
and the
Race Issue

To the Pastor

THE cure of souls—the ultimate aim of Christian ministry —is far more complex today than it was a generation or two ago. The *habitat* of the human soul, the society in which man is destined to live, work, and find the meaning of his existence, has become so complex that individuals feel lost in it—as though they had lost their bearings in some uncharted jungle.

The Race Crisis and Christian Ministry Today

Race tensions constitute one basic fact of the complex social and cultural context in which the Christian ministry is exercised, and at the same time, one of the gravest ethical issues to which the Christian gospel must address itself. Race problems are *omnipresent*, as much in lily-white suburbs as in changing neighborhoods of the "inner-city"; as much in all-Negro congregations as in the all-white congregations; as much on an Indian reservation as in a Mexican migrant-workers camp; as much among widely dispersed Japanese Americans as among highly concentrated residents of "Chinatown." Americans, irrespective of race, are in bondage to *racism*, in many cases profoundly in bondage, in others less deeply.

It will not help matters much to accuse people of harboring race prejudice, or to denounce race discrimination as a flagrant violation of Christian principles of social justice and fair play, or to reassure people that "interracial marriage" is not a serious problem because Negro men are not interested in marrying white women (or vice versa). There are white people who believe race discrimination is wrong (and unchristian), but who are nevertheless deeply disturbed by what they call the militancy of Negro people. There are Negro people who are fighting for the equality of *all* people, but who nevertheless have lost faith in the moral integrity of all white people. Neither people will be freed from such race bias by moral exhortations, nor even by scientific (biological, anthropological, sociological) analyses of the issues involved. So long as people are not liberated from "racism" of whatever shade or degree there will continue to be race tensions in society. The cure of souls in contemporary America cannot be accomplished without an emancipation of people from the racism which has engraved itself in most Americans as a kind of *second nature*.

The Races and Ethnic Groups in America

Most of us are at present preoccupied almost exclusively with the tensions and conflicts between white and Negro people. It is understandable that many white people see no difference between the problems of Negro Americans, American Indians, Japanese Americans, Spanish-speaking Americans, and so on. The pastor, however, must be more sophisticated in his understanding of different races and ethnic groups. He must be acquainted with the collective mentality (or group attitude) of various races and ethnic communities. The Negro community is fighting for its ultimate and full integration into first-class citizenship. The

American Indian community is fighting for collective survival as a nation (or nations) within American society. Americans of Asian or Latin American background are struggling to maintain their ethnic and cultural integrity while at the same time seeking full acceptance from other races and communities. Many Christians of Caucasian (white) background will accept as equals only those who have proved acceptable to them according to standards set by them. It is the pastor's responsibility to clarify the many confusions that are a part of the current race crisis.

Race: An International and Ecumenical Problem

Race problems are not a uniquely American phenomenon. The whole world is now torn by divisions of race and ethnic tradition. Within the United States race tensions are not exclusively a problem of the South or of cities with a high concentration of Negro and other ethnic groups. The problem is universal throughout the length and the breadth of this nation—North as well as South, East, West, and Midwest, literally everywhere. No village however small or remote, no suburb however exclusive, no neighborhood however tranquil, no place at all in this great land is entirely free of the race crisis.

No nation, no place, no community, and no person is really uninvolved in the problems posed by the race crisis. We in the United States must not imagine that we alone are afflicted by this problem, nor may we imagine that since the rest of the world is equally afflicted we need not take it particularly seriously. We must face the problem as it manifests itself in this country, and each pastor must face it, at his own place, and in reference to every person he encounters, beginning with himself.

The Race Crisis: A Human and a Personal Problem

Let the pastor face the problem in himself before he attempts to help others solve it. Let us emphatically understand that no one need feel shame or guilt if he discovers that he too has race prejudices of one sort or another. In the United States today literally *no one* can escape it inasmuch as everyone lives in a racially divided society. No one is born with race prejudice, but once born into a racially divided society no one is immune from it. To have prejudices is neither immoral, nor unchristian, but simply *human*, although it obviously breeds a host of immoralities and social ills.

When we find in ourselves and in others whom we love evidence of race prejudice, we should neither panic nor become defensive nor become hypercritical of others. We must face prejudice squarely for what it is. In so doing we will be facing realistically that humanity in all of us which is in need of God's grace and redemption. Race prejudice is a symptom of the sinfulness of human nature itself.

The Pastor's Ultimate Objective

The pastor's concern with race problems should be directed, primarily and finally, toward *man*, who is afflicted with race prejudice. It is not his concern to improve race relations *per se*. This does not mean the pastor should ignore the improvement of race relations in his community, state, or nation. He has a part to play in any constructive program, but that is not his *fundamental* role.

Unsound race relations are consequences of race prejudice, which in turn is, as has been pointed out, a symptom

of the sinfulness of human nature. What I wish to stress—
in fact, plead for—is that the pastor should face race prejudice, as he finds it in himself and in others, for what it is,
and deal not only with its consequences (race discrimination
and tension) but more basically with that of which it is
merely a symptom.

Such is the task which is uniquely the pastor's, and for it
there is no other profession properly equipped. The vocational discipline required is neither sociological nor psychological, but profoundly *theological*. Theology as a
discipline is vastly different from what is commonly taught
in theological seminaries, but it is precisely what is needed
in order to equip the whole Church for the cure of souls in
a society suffering from acute and chronic race tension.

The very nature of the task requires that a robust soul
undertake it. Throughout this country among pastors there
are hundreds of such robust souls—not colorful crusaders
whose statements appear frequently in the press, but
simple men of God, with firm Christian convictions, quiet
courage, steady nerve, embracing as friends all people who-
ever and whatever they are, in "faith, hope, and love." This
book should have been written by one of those heroic pastors now largely unknown to the world. With apologies for
my presumptuousness, I wish to pay tribute to them for the
great courage they display in enduring often incredible
abuse from their enemies and equally incredible misunderstanding and cynicism from their friends and colleagues.
May God grant them strength to remain faithful pastors to
the end, and may God increase the number of such pastors.

PART I

The Challenge of the Race Issue to Pastors

The Historical Background
of the Race Issue

PASSAGE of the Civil Rights Act by Congress in July, 1964, was an important landmark in the history of race relations in America. It is sobering, however, to note that it required a full century and additional legislation to spell out, if not to implement, the Emancipation Proclamation. It is even more sobering to reflect upon the many innocent lives lost, the violence perpetrated by assassins and hoodlums, the bodies maimed, the properties destroyed, the careers sacrificed—most of which suffering, though by no means all, has been inflicted upon Negro Americans.

The 1964 Civil Rights Act:
A Beginning, Not an End

The struggle for full implementation of the civil rights of all citizens regardless of race, color, or creed is far from over in this country. Those who feel Negro Americans should be content with passage of the Civil Rights Act of 1964 and should now abandon their efforts, organized or otherwise, to achieve first-class citizenship, betray how far they are out of touch with the reality of the contemporary world. The Civil Rights Act is not the end of the civil rights struggle, nor will it by itself solve the problems of racial discrimination and related problems based on race prejudice. The new legislation actually provides a tool for continuation, indeed intensification, of the civil rights struggle on the part of all sane-minded citizens—not merely members of the minority groups but *all!* By the same token —and this is the other side of the same coin—passage of the Civil Rights Act does not mean that the forces opposed to equal rights for all citizens will stop their activities. On the contrary, they are likely to intensify their activities in terms of a last-ditch struggle, and with an acute sense of desperation and even frenzy.

We must anticipate a long, drawn-out struggle, far more subtle and intense than heretofore, between the forces fighting *for* and the forces fighting *against* full implementation of the Civil Rights Act of 1964. It will be unfortunate if the forces *for* it become identified predominantly, or exclusively, with Negro Americans, and the forces *against* it with white Americans, which has so far proved pretty much the case. There are indications that an alarming proportion of white Christians of high social status, of means, and in some instances intellectual capacity oppose implementation of the Act. This puts the leadership of the Church in an extremely difficult position in that the Church itself is a "house divided against itself."

Slavery and Emancipation: The Origins of the Problem

What is happening now, however, and what will happen tomorrow, cannot be understood except against the background of what has been happening for some four centuries in America. While the current racial crisis is focused on the Negro and the white, actually race tensions in America have involved many others, notably the American Indian, in the beginnings of the nation, and more recently, the numerous immigrant communities that have made up what once was thought of as the "melting pot." It must also be remembered that the Negro in America for all too long endured one of the most pernicious forms of slavery the mind of man has yet conceived.

Slavery has existed in nearly every culture mankind has so far spawned, but never has it before been so totally identified with a particular race as has been the case with the Negro in America. It is instructive to read, in this connection, Professor Frank Tannenbaum's book, *Slave and Citizen: The Negro in the Americas.** He succinctly documents that in the Latin cultures of South America, dominated by the traditions of the Spanish and Portuguese legal system, a slave might enter his condition from any race, color, or creed, and he could also escape his condition, regardless of his race, color, or creed, by complying with certain considerations prescribed by law. In North America, however, slaves were not so fortunate. Under the peculiarities of the Anglo-Saxon legal tradition slaves were not citizens in any sense and had no civil status whatever; slaves were, in fact, property, no more and no less, owned by and entirely subject to their masters. And in North America slaves were from very early days Negroes exclusively.

Slavery started in the United States when the nation began to construct itself, and it has been inextricable from the social fabric ever since. Slave traders brought over from Africa masses of Negro people who were at once deprived of all the usual signs of personal identity—nation,

* (New York: Random House—Vintage Books, 1963).

tribe, culture, family, etc. The only identity these people were to have in their new land was that of personal property, belonging wholly to their masters, and they became that solely because they were Negroes. Slave meant Negro and Negro meant slave and the twain were never to be put asunder! A master might be fond of a slave, shower him with affection, but only as he might also behave toward a pet. The slave was never to be accorded respect and honor because he was completely deprived of human dignity. He was a Negro, no more and no other! For this reason, slaves were not permitted to marry, nor were they accorded baptism!

When such customs have built themselves into the traditions of a rapidly growing nation, it is extremely difficult later to get rid of them. To put it bluntly, to look down upon a man or a woman for no other reason than that he or she was of the Negro race, had for a long time been the *normal* (in the sense of "commonly accepted") pattern of American culture. American Christians, dominated by Anglo-Saxon Protestantism, not only failed to raise any objection, but were themselves a party to the system. Emancipation by itself did not change this situation in any significant way.* On the contrary, the rigid system of racial segregation, *de facto* as well as *de jure*, that developed after the Civil War, came into being precisely in order to preserve the effect, if not the fact, of slavery. In that system American Christians acquiesced, and only recently have they significantly objected to it.

* On this point see C. Vann Woodward, *The Strange Career of Jim Crow* (New York: Oxford University Press—Galaxy Books, 1957).

The Industrial and Urban Revolutions: Complications of the Problem

With the industrialization and urbanization of the nation, which began in the latter part of the last century and reached its climax in the years between the two world wars, the problem of race relations underwent further complication. It was inevitable for Negro Americans *en masse* to join the labor force of rapidly developing industries throughout the nation. The nation came to need Negro Americans as much as Negro Americans needed wider economic opportunities. To the majority of white Americans this required a major, indeed a radical, adjustment. Suddenly they had to accept with honor and respect Negro people as their fellow workers and neighbors! At this juncture again the voice of American Christians was neither unequivocal nor crystal clear, and the regular, churchgoing faithful were left largely to their own discretion.

During World War II the nation had a desperate need for manpower in the military services, war industries, and elsewhere. By the same time, sociological and anthropological studies had become an accepted method to introduce social changes in a peaceful and orderly manner. Every racial and ethnic minority group became an object of scientific observation, analysis, and study. American Indian reservations became stamping grounds for many budding anthropologists, and Negro Americans became the object of study by even larger numbers of sociologists. On a much smaller scale, Japanese Americans in War Relocation Centers had the distinction of being studied by both sociologists and anthropologists under "controlled" conditions —controlled in more senses than one!

Despite the great contributions such scientific studies have made—especially by taking the whole question of race relations out of the realm of personal morality and superficial sentimentality—they have also had the effect of submerging the human personality of Negro Americans (and others as well) under statistics and technical jargon. The biting comments of James Baldwin on this point deserve quotation.

One of the reasons we are so fond of sociological reports and research and investigational committees is because they hide something. As long as we can deal with the Negro as a kind of statistic, as something to be manipulated, something to be fled from, or something to be given something to, there is something we can avoid and what we can avoid is what he really, really means to us.*

We have discovered new and more sophisticated ways to ignore the personal identities of Negro Americans, and we have all become much too accustomed to the new ways to be free from their ill effects.

For these and other reasons to which reference will be made later, for most white Americans Negro Americans have been and still are strangers—almost total strangers. Americans of other ethnic backgrounds, be they Oriental or Spanish-speaking Americans, American Indians, or recent immigrants from other foreign countries, have something other than their race with which they can be identified. They are different from Anglo-Saxon white Americans, but their difference is not solely on the basis of race, but also of language, culture, and not least, their old countries! Or,

* James Baldwin, *Nobody Knows My Name* (New York: Dial, 1961), p. 135.

again, most white Americans have far less difficulty relating themselves to contemporary Africans who visit America in increasing numbers nowadays, because they are citizens of one recognized nation or another, besides being of Negro race, and their national identity at once explains why they are strangers among us and motivates us to treat them as "guests."

For the Negro American, however, his strangeness is solely and exclusively on account of his being Negro—in every other respect he is just as much American as any other citizen! Simply because of his race he has been kept apart, and consequently has not been known through direct, person-to-person encounter, dialogue, and association, on any continuing basis. Yet the fact remains that he *is* one of us, he *is* among us and *is* with us, unknown to us (though suspected of knowing us well), so close to us yet so far from us, having no other homeland but this, no other mother tongue but American English, and having done his share of the work which has made America what she is! If other Americans cannot accept him as a neighbor and a friend, simply because he has for some reason remained a stranger, they are bound to feel guilty, and to be threatened by his presence. To most white Americans, Christians not excepted, negro-ness has been uncritically accepted as the reason Negroes are strangers in their midst. Once this is established, what happens to Negro Americans ceases to be any concern of white Americans. Such has been the case to this day, and American Christians, far from protesting against it, have been parties to it, and often champions of it.

If white Americans have turned Negro Americans into strangers, the nation as a whole, dominated by the North, has turned the South into something of a "foreign" land.

European colonial powers were able to "solve" their race problems by confining them to far-away colonies (which is the reason England has until recently had little racial tension). In the same way, America has attempted to "solve" her race problem by pretending it was confined to the South, and that all responsibility belonged to the South. This is one reason so many white Christians, especially in the North, have thus far failed to face the problem squarely and seriously—they have convinced themselves that the problem is not theirs but the southerners'! How untenable this position is has been well expressed in a fable related by the late Dr. Charles Johnson, President of Fisk University:

A Negro lad who grew up in a little Mississippi town had been hearing about the great dividing line between the North and the South of the United States called the Mason-Dixon line. One day he decided to see it himself and set out on a journey northward eagerly looking for this famous line, but before he found any sign of it he found himself at the Canadian border!

The North is as much involved in the South as the South in the North. The race problem in America is mainly *in the minds* of white Americans, and it is there that the problem has to be met. This means that the race problem specifically includes people living in lily-white suburbs in the North! The Negro as a *collective image* is present in the mind of every white American today, and if he knows no Negro, or has never met a Negro in the flesh, the Negro image living in his mind is likely to be so much the more hideous. Such a white American, reading or hearing about Negroes like Martin Luther King, Jr., James Farmer, Roy Wilkins, Whitney Young, Philip Randolph, Thurgood

Marshall, or even Ralph Bunche, cannot *see* them as individual persons but only as *the Negro!*

Let us, then, at the outset frankly acknowledge the indefatigable and statesmanlike leadership of a succession of Negro lawyers, educators, churchmen, and social workers, and the inestimable contribution of a variety of civic organizations. Without their efforts and the assistance they received from enlightened white and other racial leaders, race relations in America today would be far more strained than they are. When we pay tribute to the high moral quality, the integrity, and the statesmanship of these pioneers, we do not forget the many nameless men and women, young people (and even children), both Negro and white, particularly in the South, who really are the unsung heroes, dead or alive, of the long drawn-out struggle for racial justice in this great land. Does it not illustrate how much wiser God's foolishness is than man's wisdom (1 Cor. 1:25), that God has raised up a succession of indomitable champions of social justice from among the victims of a social injustice almost unprecedented in history? This above all is why the Church must accept the challenge of the race crisis as a central concern of Christian ministry.

Japanese Americans and American Indians: Other Examples of the Problem

What I have said about the collective image of the Negro living in every white American's mind is partly the reflection of an experience I had during World War II. I am, it happens, a Japanese American. Having been officially branded "aliens unassimilable to United States society" by Act of Congress in 1924, we Japanese Americans had become something of an enigma to most other Americans. We were personally discriminated against and socially segregated. When war broke out between the United States and Japan, therefore, it was natural that the presence of Japanese Americans in the United States was considered a dangerous menace.

The now infamous mass "relocation" of Japanese Americans was perhaps inevitable. We—110,000 of us—were locked up behind barbed-wire fences, securely guarded by military sentries. Within a short time the Japanese American as a collective image was more vivid in the minds of white Americans throughout the nation. This was especially true on the Pacific Coast, where Japanese Americans had lived for years as neighbors, customers, farmers, or businessmen. Most of them had children in the public schools attended by other children. The situation after the "relocation" was much worse than before: The demon chased out of the house returned with seven other and more fierce companions. Japanese Americans in the flesh could be confined to a restricted corner of society, but Japanese Americans as an image became omnipresent, and appeared unspeakably hideous to the eyes of fear-ridden minds. Likewise, within the so-called "relocation center" Japanese Americans were similarly haunted by a collective image of the white American! Very soon the appointed personnel of the War Relocation Authority and even visiting missionaries and representatives of American churches —emissaries of good will—came to be seen only in terms of that image. They were all *the white man*, and therefore categorically assumed to be hostile toward Japanese Americans.

When American Indians were "put away" into reservations, much the same mixture of fear and guilt on the part of white Americans was internalized. What was thought to be the menace of savage Indians did not by any means end. It was, in fact, perpetuated. In neither of these national experiences did the old saying "out of sight, out of mind" prove true. It is reported that an automatic translation machine once rendered this old saying into Chinese as "blind and mad." The error of the machine comes closer to the truth. There is more than a touch of blindness and madness in white Americans who think they can successfully hide people of different races behind barbed-wire fences, or on reservations, or even behind statistics.

The Supreme Court Decision of 1954: Facing-up to the Problem

During the last twenty-five years many developments have tended to bring the race issue in America into a much sharper focus. Probably the most dramatic, and in some ways the most historic, was the decision by the Supreme Court on May 17, 1954, that segregation in the public schools is unconstitutional. Since that decision the movement toward desegregation has been steadily growing, not only in public schools but in many other areas of national life as well.

Two earlier developments, both during World War II, had done much to arouse the public conscience with respect to race problems. The first, discussed above, was the mass "relocation" of people of Japanese descent, citizens and aliens alike, from the Pacific Coast in 1942, at the time American forces were fighting against the racism of Nazi Germany. The second was the race riots in Detroit during the summer of 1943, first of the major race incidents in northern cities.

Following the 1954 decision, leadership of the civil rights movement was, for some years, largely concentrated among a few public-spirited citizens and professional human relations workers. Prior to the decision there had been intensive and untiring effort by groups such as the National Association for the Advancement of Colored People, the Southern Regional Council, the Annual Race Relations Institute (begun in 1944 at Fisk University) sponsored by the American Missionary Association, the Department of Racial and Cultural Relations of the National (formerly Federal) Council of Churches of Christ in the U.S.A., and others, which collectively prepared the groundwork and climate for the historic decision of the Supreme Court. Notable also among pioneer efforts were the several "freedom rides" undertaken prior to May, 1954, by the Congress of Racial Equality.

The experience of Negro servicemen overseas during World War I, especially in France, may be said to have introduced a significant new departure in the history of Negro-white relationships in America. During World War II, however, more important developments took place, including desegregation of the armed forces; for the first time Negro soldiers fought, were wounded, and died side by side with white and other soldiers. Those Negro soldiers who survived to return to civilian life make up a large part of the "new" Negroes of today. They are no longer content, because of the wartime experience, with second-class citizenship.

Another major new departure in the civil rights struggle was the mass boycott of buses by Negro citizens in Montgomery, Alabama, which lasted nearly a year starting in late 1955. This boycott made Dr. Martin Luther King,

Jr., a principal figure in the civil rights movement. The participation of the masses of Negroes in the struggle was given further impetus by the "sit-in" demonstrations started by college students in Greensboro, North Carolina, in February, 1960. By 1964, the civil rights movement had taken on the proportions of a mass revolution, and for the first time ordinary Negro citizens were taking a very active part. The great majority of Negroes seem now united in a common purpose—to realize full rights of citizenship without delay. This purpose is expressed in the familiar slogan: "Freedom now!"

Although alarmed in different ways by all of these events, the white community has been very slow to respond to the demands of Negro citizens. The striking contrast between the thoroughness of discipline, group organization, and alertness of leadership on the part of the Negro Christian community and the almost total lack of responsible action on the part of the white Christian community in Montgomery, Alabama, during and following the bus boycott, is indicative of a fundamental difference in outlook between the Negro and white communities. This difference has accentuated a feeling of frustration and impatience on the part of Negro citizens, rapidly developing into a loss of confidence in white leadership.

A New Situation: At Home and Abroad

Revolutionary changes in the political situation, first in Asia and later in Africa after World War II, and the acceleration of industrialization in America, brought about a radically new context for Negro-white relationships in America. Despite this, the great significance of the Bandung Conference of Asian-African nations in 1955 went largely unnoticed by official circles in the United States.

"Washington failed either to anticipate what would happen at Bandung or to accept what did happen." The then Secretary of State referred to it merely as the "*so-called* Asian-African conference," and "whereas Russia and Canada sent greetings, the United States said nothing. The lone U.S. congressman present was obliged to attend as a newspaperman," reported Winburn Thomas, then a missionary to Indonesia.*

At home, meanwhile, the "rural exodus" of southern Negroes, begun during the interwar years, had been greatly accelerated during World War II, when the general manpower shortage and especially the shortage of skilled workers and professionally trained people opened up new employment opportunities for Negro and other ethnic groups. (In this situation the Federal Government exercised decisive leadership.) Ever since, and especially in the South, technical skills and industrial productivity have been at a premium, and Negro citizens are now, though still under great handicaps, competing with white and other citizens in a market which is increasingly open.

Overseas, during the same years, new nations have been emerging at unprecedented speed in Asia and Africa, most of which, with few exceptions, have taken their rightful places in the United Nations as self-respecting independent nation-states. The Negro citizens of the United States have begun to fear that all of Negro Africa will be free long before all American Negroes attain first-class citizenship.

It is no wonder, then, that the fight of American Negroes for civil and human rights has passed the point of no return. They are pushed from behind by all that has happened at

* *Christian Century*, May 11, 1955.

home in the last eventful decades, and simultaneously pulled ahead by the example of many nations abroad moving rapidly toward freedom and "the promised land." American Negroes today are confident of themselves as never before, united, courageous, and determined.

1311793

Race Segregation: An Anachronism

Seen in this context, all attempts to keep one people separated from, let alone subjugated to, another people solely on the basis of race, color, ethnic origin, or religion, whether by legislation or by perpetuating established social customs or habits, has become a historical anachronism. There are white people in America, in no small number at that, who, being possessed of considerable power—political, economic and social—either refuse or fail to be contemporary with the times in which they live. These people have difficulty in comprehending that racial discrimination is immoral, because it has for years been built into their mores and into the very structure of their society. The problem is theological as well as moral in that it involves a refusal to acknowledge God's work in history.

Nowadays Afro-Asian peoples learn within a matter of hours of desperate attempts made by white people to maintain old patterns of race segregation in America. Negro citizens in America learn just as quickly of the many vestiges of white colonial imperialism abroad, and of the last-ditch battle to keep alive what little is left of it in the Afro-Asian world. Furthermore, there exist in the world undemocratic forces that do not fail to capitalize on these events to turn people of colored races against democracy. Therefore, we must soberly face the fact that the racial conflict within the United States has far-reaching ramifications in terms of the moral and cultural leadership of the democratic nations in an emerging "one world."

The New Negro and the Survival of Democracy

The line of demarcation between *domestic* and *foreign* has been all but obscured in the contemporary world. It is against this background that we must seek to understand Negro leadership in America and the peculiar problems and responsibilities it confronts. Most Negro leaders today are found in religious, legal, educational, or academic professions as well as in social welfare and action groups. They include first-rate intellectuals and persons of high moral integrity, and with very few exceptions are firmly committed to the principles of constitutional democracy. As Professor Franklin Littel said in his address at the Religion and Race Conference in Chicago, in January, 1963, we cannot thank God enough that they are. These Negro leaders are, and have been for years, determined to achieve their aims exclusively by democratic means—that is, within the framework of constitutional law.

Underlying their much discussed nonviolence is a commitment to democratic principles and a determination to abide by them. For this reason they accept jail sentences when constrained to break laws of states or cities which deny them their civil rights. They are, in other words, compelled to challenge the constitutional and moral validity of undemocratic laws, and to do so in the name of democracy even at the risk of imprisonment. So long as such laws remain on the books, however unconstitutional, they are willing to take the consequences of breaking them. Here the law is being judged just as they are being judged by the law.

Appreciating with gratitude the moral caliber and intellectual quality of Negro leaders, we must also have sympathy for them in the almost hopeless situations they confront in many parts of the United States. The power structures of state and local communities are frequently controlled by people whose outlook and behavior are basically opposed to the establishment of justice for all citizens. Such conduct and behavior resemble that of colonial dictators, and are so regarded by a growing number of Negro citizens.

While new Afro-Asian nations are struggling to be fully emancipated from all vestiges of colonialism, Negro citizens in America are making desperate efforts to complete their own emancipation from the vestiges of slavery. Moreover, as described earlier, this movement has become a "revolt of the masses" against the established system, and the leadership alone can no longer wholly control its trend and direction. The same difficulty, then, faces Negro leadership in America as faces the leadership of nationalist movements in Africa today. Both are caught between the anachronism of an established power structure and the impatience of the masses who are following and pushing them at the same time.

One of the impressive facts of contemporary history is that despite the injustices and indignities so long inflicted upon them by white people, Negro leaders in America and in Africa have so far largely ignored overtures made to them by antidemocratic forces in the world. It is not an exaggeration to say that democratic principles appear to have taken deeper roots in Negro communities than in white or other racial or ethnic communities. It may be that the Negro people have learned how "power corrupts" from the standpoint of victims of a power that has absolutized itself.

Thus conceived the fight of American Negroes for civil rights is nothing less than the struggle for democracy to survive and mature. There are people in the United States (both in the North and in the South), as there are in the Republic of South Africa, who believe that the current race crisis is really a crisis of the survival of "white" civilization. That such is not the case seems evident, and will not be argued here. More important is to argue that failure to accord Negro citizens full civil rights in America is tantamount to a breakdown of democracy itself, which could have world-wide ramifications. No one is truly free until all are free.

"Community of the Hurt . . ."

It is, therefore, hardly surprising that there has developed a deep sense of kinship between African nationalists and American Negro civil rights leaders. They have come to identify with each other *less* on the basis of common racial ancestry and *more* because they are fighting for one and the same cause. This, I believe, is the real meaning of what is commonly referred to as the solidarity of the Afro-Asian peoples, as expressed in the unforgettable words of General Carlos Romulo of the Philippines at Bandung, in 1955: "We belong to the community of the hurt, and heartbroken and of deferred hope." *

* *Christian Century*, May 11, 1955.

Granting both legitimacy and validity to the demands of Negro citizens, many still ask, "Why such a rush?" It must be pointed out that those who are not Negro probably have little conception of what it is like to be a Negro today in the United States. *De facto* segregation in the North and legally constituted segregation in the South over the years have virtually prohibited genuine, heart-to-heart communication between Negro and other citizens.

Historically those in power have seldom taken the time to listen to, much less to understand, what oppressed or subjugated people have to say. "Let the people obey, never be listened to" (the motto of the Tokugawa Shogunate in Japan) is more often than not the code of those in power. Wittingly and unwittingly American Christians outside the Negro community have followed this widely accepted code of behavior without criticism. Consequently, white Christian citizens still are unable to *hear* what Negro Christian citizens are saying.

This is the crux of the current racial crisis in the United States. What American Negroes are demanding is what a majority of Afro-Asian people have already secured from their former colonial masters. Even a cursory reading of the Civil Rights Act of 1964 makes this point crystal clear. Yet there are many white Christians who think that Negro citizens are demanding far too much and trying to get all of it much too fast. This kind of thinking, if it may be called "thinking" at all, comes from the fact that otherwise reasonably decent white Christians are incapable of looking at themselves in the perspective of the contemporary world, and are quite incapable of hearing what their Negro neighbors are saying.

It is imperative that American Christians perceive the

racial implications of the troubles manifested overseas, for example in Panama, Zanzibar, and Kenya. To say that these disturbances are caused by Communist agitation not only betrays superficiality of observation but is also downright irresponsible. It fails to take into account undeniable historical facts. Panama, for instance, has been the single exception among Latin American countries in that it is the only one where "citizens are publicly barred or affronted on the grounds of Negro or Indian (or any other) ancestry." * At a time when nationalism is a vital force undergirding the Latin American social and cultural revolution, it would be astonishing if Panamanians did not resent the racial discrimination which has been imposed upon them by the United States. The question of exactly what did precipitate the present tensions is immaterial to an understanding of the true nature of the problem. By the same token, in most Afro-Asian countries a political regime which has identified, wrongly or rightly, with former colonial rulers is likely to be opposed by racially conscious nationalists.

American Negroes have, in summary, more and more realized that their struggle for full freedom in the United States is historically bound up with a world-wide revolution. This growing identity of interest between leaders of the struggle in America and leaders of the struggle in Africa and Asia and throughout the world may be the most important development of the decade 1960-1970. The implications not only politically as we move closer toward "one world," but also ecumenically as we move

* J. Halcro Ferguson, *Latin America: The Balance of Race Redressed* (London: Oxford University Press, for Institute of Race Relations, 1961), p. 81.

closer to reunion of the Christian Church, are worth pondering. The Christian ministry, after all, is especially a ministry to the "community of the hurt," and that community extends around the world.

2

The Race Issue
and the Ministry of Christ

THE question before us is what, if anything, should the Church be doing while the bitter struggle continues and intensifies between forces *for* and forces *against* the full implementation of civil rights for all citizens. Obviously, the Church cannot defer action until all her members are agreed upon every detail of race relations. Nor can the Church ignore the fact that there are at present profound differences of view about the race issue within its membership. What, then, can the Church do *now*, even as a "house divided"?

Pastoral Responsibility

But before this question can be answered, we must consider the prior question which many pastors put this way: "What really does the race issue have to do with the ministry of Christ?"

I am myself a Christian minister, and, I trust, think as one. Moreover, it is to Christian ministers primarily, although not exclusively, that I speak here. It is my belief that the race issue is crucial to the ministry of Christ in contemporary America. It is, therefore, my contention that the ministry must devote itself wholeheartedly to the challenge presented by the race crisis, not as an extracurricular or marginal concern of the ministry, but precisely as a fundamental preoccupation. I mean this especially as it applies to the pastoral ministry—that is, to the minister charged with responsibility for a local congregation. Let us now enumerate the reasons why I think race relations are a central problem for the Church and its pastoral ministry.

1. MINISTRY TO THE WORLD MEANS MINISTRY IN THE WORLD. The society in which we live, and to which we minister, is a society profoundly torn by racial conflict. Few of the great social changes of our time, at home or abroad, can be separated from the race issue. As we have seen, for example, there is the "integration," economical and industrial, of the old South ever more deeply into the fabric of the American nation. Those Christians, then, who now resist desegregation are, sad to say, still living in a bygone past, and seem emotionally unable to accept the present as a reality.

The ministry of the Church to modern man—white or Negro, segregationist or integrationist, progressive or reactionary, liberal or conservative, indifferent or apathetic —is, as a matter of fact, taking place within the context of a society in which there is no longer any significant difference between North and South, East and West. (Even the demarcation between domestic and foreign is rapidly becoming obscure and may eventually be obliterated.) The ministry of Christ can be relevant and effective only if it meets the needs of the whole man *within the context* of this urbanized and industrialized society that is nationwide. It is not race relations *per se* with which the Church must deal but with the reality of contemporary society, which is the *habitat* of modern man's soul. Racial tensions, properly understood, can throw light on this total ministry.

2. BIBLICAL THEOLOGY IS EXISTENTIAL: RACE IS A FACT OF LIFE. Basic Christian doctrine, notably the Fall and original sin, is radically illuminated within the context of race tensions. It is possible, of course, to consider Christian doctrine in the abstract, and theological scholars properly do so, but for most of us, and perhaps for pastors especially, the familiar doctrines only come alive when we confront them in concrete historical and social situations. Who can fail to see original sin powerfully at work in the contemporary race crisis? Who can deny the Fall when he faces the awful alienation, the unspeakable violence and hate, the division of peoples, of communities, and, yes, even of congregations? We cannot understand, indeed, we cannot make sense out of this terrible national scandal without placing it in the context of the Christian teaching about evil.

Christian doctrine, let it be noted, aims to provide answers to the questions man has asked out of the depth of his anguish, in a life filled with contradiction and inconsistency—yes, with injustice, unfairness, ugliness and hopelessness. How is he to make sense of his existence? Does it make sense that he try to make an honest living against all odds in this fallen world? Why should he not have the liberty to do as he pleases or to quit when he feels that he can no longer carry on? In answer to these and related questions, raised not for the sake of philosophical argument but from the depth of the agony of existence, Christian theology ventures to speak in statements such as: "In the beginning, God created. . . . And, behold, it was good."

Or, "God was in Christ reconciling the world unto himself. . . ." Only when heard as answers, do these and other statements in the Bible make sense, and never otherwise.

This great nation, by far the richest and most powerful of all the nations of the world, was founded upon convictions that have become the envy of mankind: "All men are created equal, endowed with certain unalienable rights, among which are life, liberty and the pursuit of happiness." America has come to conceive of herself as "the last, best hope" to prove that "government of the people, by the people, and for the people" not only works but is the best form of government man has devised. How are these convictions to be maintained in the face of the race crisis that has come upon us? Are we not compelled to take a new look at the nature of man and the nature of society in the light of biblical revelation and the gospel?

Throughout the world we see other societies similarly challenged by race conflict and tension. We think most often, perhaps, of the Republic of South Africa, of other parts of Africa and Asia, where the race question has been bound up with colonialism and recently with the independence movement among the developing nations. Actually, however, the race problem surrounds the globe, and there is no nation, no people, no society, that is not radically touched by it.

Nevertheless, considered in the light of the principles upon which the United States was founded and built, it is peculiarly hard to explain how, in the last half of the twentieth century, there should be in America such shocking—brutal, savage, violent, hellish—conflicts between races of people. It is tempting to try to account for it in terms of some terrible sickness that has come upon us, but, as Christians, must we not look instead for the answer which is found in the doctrine of original sin?

Speaking of the specific problem of the South in the light of history, James Baldwin has written:

> The North, in winning the war, left the South only one means of asserting its identity and that means was the Negro. . . . In sum, the North, by freeing the slaves of their masters, robbed the masters of any possibility of freeing themselves of the slaves.*

This statement is a kind of phenomenology, or description, of original sin, and strongly implies that any adequate answer to the agonizing question of race in modern America must be theological. And the task of the Church is not merely to improve race relations. It is not less than what it has always been: to save souls.

3. "YOU SHALL LOVE YOUR NEIGHBOR AS YOURSELF": THE MEANING OF FREEDOM.   A man's soul cannot be saved in the abstract, apart from his social environment, nor can it be saved merely by improving or reconstructing that environment. This is a fact of theology just as true in America as in any other place. Nor can a man save his own soul by education, by "will power," or by learning to "adjust" to his environment. To be saved a man's soul must, according to Christian theology, become whole, and this "wholeness" implies, among other things, wholesome relationships with others, a wholesome relationship with one's social environment. And social environment for each one of us means the people we live among, our neighbors, without any regard

* James Baldwin, *Nobody Knows My Name* (New York: Dial, 1961), pp. 123-24.

whatever to race, color, religious persuasion, or ethnic origin.

By translating the language of theology into the language of the social sciences, we can say that salvation depends upon integration of the personality, and integration of the personality upon "integration" of the person into society. Salvation is not possible except a man be in wholesome relationship with his fellow man—all of his fellow men, everywhere in this world.

Therefore, man is fulfilled only in his relationships with other people, only within the context of the contemporary world—not in the world to come, nor in the world that was! Man cannot love God with all his heart, mind, soul, and might, apart from loving his neighbor as himself. Nor can he love his neighbor as himself unless he is capable of loving himself.

Careful reading of the letters of Paul and John makes clear that love is not a moral virtue to be attained by man, but primarily a dynamic force (or, as Mahatma Gandhi would have put it, "soul-force") that creates and sustains relationships. The opposite of love is hate, and hate is a force which impairs and destroys relationships, depriving men of the opportunity to be persons. To hate is to kill, nothing less. To live is to love; and not to love is death. "We know that we have passed out of death into life because we love the brethren. He who does not love remains in death. Any one who hates his brother is a murderer . . ." (1 John 3:14-15, RSV).

This is exactly what we are learning painfully as we experience the racial issues of our day within our own society. No one is under any obligation to like or to take to his bosom races other than his own. How can one love a race? Nor is anyone commanded to be affectionate toward another person merely because he is of a different race. What is required of each one of us is that he live *in relation with* every other person who comes within the range of his life. There is nothing morally virtuous about this, any more than it is virtuous to live according to natural law. It is a question of living by "the law of liberty" (James 1:25, RSV), "the law that set us free" (NEB); and one may defy it or walk against it only at his own risk and ultimately at the expense of his freedom.

Yet before our eyes in broad daylight all over the United States presumably intelligent and decent men and women, often in all sincerity, are trying to defy this very "law of liberty" in the name of freedom! Freedom is defined in extraordinary ways and the number of definitions is legion: states rights, freedom of association, the right to restrict customers or clientele to those of one's own choosing, the maintenance of "racial purity" (whatever this may mean). In the name of freedom elaborate collective actions are being taken, ostensibly to resist intervention by the government; but in reality these actions are unlawful, and despite their being voluntary freedom is crushed to pieces.

The sad fact is that substantial numbers of churchgoing Christians participate overtly or covertly in these strange tactics. They do so sincerely, apparently convinced that their actions are compatible with democracy, and—even more astonishing—compatible with the Christian message. They seem oblivious of the fact that their actions amount to collective homicide and suicide. It is not at all unreasonable to suggest that, projected onto a world scale, such actions may bring about the extermination of mankind.

How, in the name of Christ, can the Church remain silent or refrain from active protest, when confronted by such evil in its midst?

Few Americans, Christians certainly not excluded, have grasped the meaning of freedom, either in its political sense as defined in the historic papers of the United States, or in its religious sense as defined in the Christian gospel. American churches have for many years sent missionaries around the world, and in the days of slavery they did not neglect to send missionaries among the slaves. Perhaps the time has come for the churches to send their missionaries into their own congregations!

The ministry of Christ is profoundly, directly, powerfully, and inescapably challenged by the race crisis in America.

What Are Pastors to Do?

Having established the relationship of the race issue to the Christian ministry, we are now ready to discuss what can be done.

The step which most readily suggests itself to many pastors is to set about to integrate immediately church institutions and congregations. This is an important and significant step, but we need to be very clear about its meaning, and we have to ask ourselves whether this in itself constitutes the major task of the pastoral ministry.

Obviously it is not enough for each local church to announce to the world that its door is open to all people regardless of race, color, or ethnic origin—although many have not done even this much. Nor is it enough for each denominational body to close its heretofore "Negro" institutions and congregations. When that is proposed it must be simultaneously asked whether American Indian, Chinese, Japanese, Filipino, Mexican, and Puerto Rican congregations are to be disbanded.

I personally am not persuaded that such an approach is necessarily sound, even to advance the cause of race integration. It is questionable that integration is promoted when all-white congregations receive into their midst certain numbers of Negro and other nonwhite Christians. This approach to integration in itself betrays the arrogance of many still unrepentant white Christians. It does not differ in nature from the opposite position which advocates segregation because "they want to be with their own people." In either case, "solutions" are arrived at by white Christians strictly on their own terms ("we receive them into our midst"), and no one thinks to ask Negro Christians what they might think of it. The fact is, however, that nine out of ten white Christians see nothing wrong with either "solution."

It is, nevertheless, disgrace enough that so many white American congregations (while generously supporting missionary work in Africa) are painfully slow to accept Negro Christians into their membership, or Negro clergy into their pastoral ministry. Disgraceful, but hardly surprising, when we consider that it may be argued that segregation has its origins within the churches. Discussing C. Vann Woodward's *The Strange Career of Jim Crow*, Kyle Haselden has pointed out:

First came the segregation of the Negro within the Church; then followed the separation of the churches by the "spontaneous" withdrawal of the Negro Christians; much later, the elaborate patterns of segregation were to arise in the church and in secular society. Long before the little signs—"White only" and "Colored"—appeared in the public utilities they had appeared in the church.*

The churches, then, bearing as they do heavy responsibility for the existence of segregation in America, certainly must proceed with no less than "all deliberate speed" to desegregate their own congregations and institutions.

At the same time I do not believe it to be either creative or helpful for the leadership of the Church to be so exclusively preoccupied with the matter of the desegregation of congregations. There are many other tasks that the Church and the ministry can do and ought to be doing in the name of the Master and in the light of the Gospel. These tasks have been neglected for far too long a period, and we need to discuss some of them here.

First, congregational (or corporate) worship should be something more and basically other than a mere cult of congeniality. The sermon should be more than an echo of the voice of the world or a mere moral exhortation couched in biblical language—it should proclaim the mighty act of God in history. Pastoral counseling should prescribe something more than "peace of mind." Parish activities should aspire to more than mutual edification and social pleasure. Indeed, this lack of attention to the basic functions of the ministry is responsible for the apathy of churchgoing white Christians when they are confronted by the injustices, humiliations, and indignities suffered by Negro Americans.

Consider the paradoxical situation which has resulted from this. The victims of incomprehensible injustice, having been denied lawful means to register a protest against,

* Kyle Haselden, *The Racial Problem in Christian Perspective* (New York: Harper & Row, 1959), p. 29.

let alone remove, the injustice, are now *called upon*—and I say "called upon" advisedly and emphatically, because they are called upon by history—to take the initiative to correct the injustice they have for·generations endured. Having taken the initiative, and with determination not to resort to violence but only to peaceful and democratic means, they are met more often than not with indifference and cynicism on the part of society at large. Not infrequently they are labeled "extremists," "agitators," and what all, while the masses within their own communities grow daily more and more impatient and restless. How can the Church, whose sons and daughters they are, be so naïve as to give them merely counsel of moderation and patience?

Allow me to introduce a parable in the form of a personal experience. In 1943 I took a two-month leave from the relocation center to which I was then assigned and went around the country speaking to many groups. At one place a woman said to me, "Mr. Kitagawa, you are not really Japanese, are you?" "Yes, I am, but why do you question it?" I retorted. "Because," she said with a smile all over her face, "you are too good looking to be a Japanese." (This, I might add, is the one and only occasion, the first and last time in my life that I have been complimented for my looks!) This, I believe, is a parable—a parable of destereotyping, so to speak. During World War II the United States, having made a historic mistake in the mass evacuation of people of Japanese descent from the West Coast, also manifested greatness and magnanimity in allowing a Japanese national like myself to appear *in person* before all sorts of groups, that is, all segments of the general public, and to state the case of Japanese Americans. Should not Negro Americans today have this same freedom? I believe the United States is as great today as she was in 1943, in the crisis of World War II, and capable of being as magnanimous with Negro Americans now as she was with Japanese Americans then.

In view of the difficulties and paradoxes which the Church faces, it is quite understandable that many pastors feel frustrated when confronted by the race issue. Frequently, they find themselves in this dilemma: if they say nothing, they are accused of indifference and cowardice; if they say something, they are accused of hypocrisy or of meddling—either way they run the risk of losing or driving away "stanch supporters" of the Church.

What then are pastors to do? Where are they to begin if they are not to be exclusively (and pathologically) preoccupied with desegregation, on the one hand, or on the other, to be satisfied with the repetition of pious platitudes or organizing a series of innocuous study groups? What can be done within the regular framework of their ministry, in season and out of season, seven days a week?

To sketch just such a pastoral program is the purpose of this book. We shall not attempt here to offer final answers to all questions or to all phases of the race issue. But we are concerned to offer all pastors the opportunity to engage in a disciplined process of thought and action on the race issue, which is, in the final analysis, the problem of man.

I am convinced that this problem, at once so acute and so urgent, so complex and so intense, requires that rarest of all combinations, a warm heart and a cool head. It also requires an equally rare combination of personal commitment and collective action. No movement of uncommitted individuals will do, nor will lone crusaders, however dedicated, suffice. Organized collective action on the part of thoroughly committed individuals, striking at strategic points at the most opportune moments, is the only answer.

Early in 1944 at a meeting of the then Federal Council of Churches' Committee on Japanese American Resettlement, Dr. Joseph Hunter, former missionary to Japan, and at that time a relocation officer in Arizona, said, "It is a serious matter for one American citizen to question the loyalty of another American citizen." This statement has stuck in my mind all these years.

By the same token, and in fact much more urgently, it is intolerable—a sin, a crime, an offense, call it what you will—for one Christian not to accept and not to be accepted by another Christian, at the Communion rail, in the pew, in the Bible class, in the neighborhood meeting, or in any other place. This is the crucial, and perhaps the only, issue the Church confronts. As Christians, and more particularly as ministers in whom the responsibility of leadership of the Church is vested, let us remember that our task is not less or other than, "the ministry of reconciliation" (2 Cor. 5:18).

PART II

Pastoral
Preaching

3

Christian Preaching
on the Race Issue

MANY pastors on reading the title of this chapter may well exclaim: "Enough of preaching! What we need is not more words but action." My feeling, however—and it is based almost entirely on hunch—is that most sermons on race relations preached from the pulpits of Protestant churches are mainly *moral exhortations* to abide by the Supreme Court decision or by the law of the land. Will Campbell neatly put his finger on this approach when he noted that "Thus saith the Law" has replaced "Thus saith the Lord." If it is this kind of preaching to which some pastors take exception, I join with them: "Enough of pious platitudes expressed in biblical terminology and of pep talks for social action."

Still another approach to preaching is this. A pastor, usually young, will preach a sermon on race relations largely to inform his congregation *where he stands*. This might be called the "position-taking" sermon. Having once preached such a sermon ("Come what may, here I stand. I can do no other!"), the pastor is often obliged to spend his energies "defending" that position, perhaps even causing his congregation to split into factions, pro, con, indifferent.

Now it should be clear that neither of these approaches has to do really with Christian preaching in the sense of *proclaiming the gospel*—that is, of proclaiming the good news, "God is in Christ reconciling the world to himself" (2 Cor. 5:18 f.). Therefore, we shall not attempt here to tell the pastor how or what to preach on race relations, but we shall focus our attention solely on the gospel and its implications for the contemporary race crisis.

The Proclamation of God's Mighty Act in History

In Christian preaching it is our duty to proclaim the mighty act of God himself—not in the past tense, nor in the future tense, nor yet in the subjunctive or conditional mood, but *in the present tense* and *in the indicative mood!* God has in Christ reconciled the world to himself once and for all. What does this mean in the context of the contemporary race crisis? Certainly it is not apart from these acute racial tensions that God is reconciling the world to himself. Nor does it mean that when and if the race conflict is resolved, God will accept the world once again as his own. What *is* meant is that "God who in *everything* works for good with those who love him" (Rom. 8:28, RSV) is now working through his Church *in the midst of race tensions* to bring the estranged world of men back to himself. The Church is being called upon to participate in the divine ministry of reconciliation which has been initiated by Jesus Christ through his life, death, and resurrection.

This is *at the heart* of Christian preaching on race relations. Far too often, however, one hears from the pulpit a capsule discourse on the "races of mankind" based on high school biology and social anthropology textbooks. What an insult to the intelligence of men and women in the pew, and what an adulteration of preaching! Paul did say that God chose to save those who believe by "the foolishness of preaching" (1 Cor. 1:21, AV), but he did not mean to say, by "foolish preaching." "The folly of what we preach" (RSV) is not *our* folly in misunderstanding what preaching really is!

The Context in Which We Preach

God's act to reconcile the world to himself does not take place in a vacuum. The world he is reconciling to himself is no mere abstract concept or mental construct of philosophers and theologians, but the world as it really is, in which you and I are living, in which all manner of evil, wrong, and injustice are found, and which at the present moment is torn asunder by acute race conflict and tension. To put it in more personal terms, man's (personal) salvation cannot take place in a vacuum, but only *within the context* of and *in reference to* present reality. That reality today obviously includes race tension and division. Salvation of an individual man or woman, in other words, cannot be found in his or her being taken out of "this crooked generation" or world (cf. Acts 2:40), but only by their remaining a part of God's people in the world—the people chosen by God for the purpose of redeeming the otherwise irredeemable world (cf. John 17:15-19).

Christian preaching cannot afford to treat the race crisis as though it did not exist. It is, at the very least, part of the social and cultural context in which modern man "lives, moves and has his being." As such it constitutes a frame of reference within which all other moral problems, however personal in nature, can be dealt with realistically. The context (or frame of reference) in which we preach is not, of course, the subject matter (or content) of our sermons. Rather, it is the stage-setting as it were, in which we perform our role. What is central, and indeed essential, is the performance. Every word we speak is heard and evaluated against the background and scenery of the stage from which we speak.

The Race Crisis: The Context of Contemporary Preaching

When we proclaim the gospel that "God has in Christ reconciled the world to himself," we do so in the context of race conflict. In more personal terms, we preach out of the context of our own hostility toward other people based upon their race or ethnic origin. Personal salvation (or redemption of the world) cannot be accomplished apart from the race and ethnic tensions which penetrate every aspect of modern life the world over.

Suppose we try to expound the meaning of the Ten Commandments and of Christ's summary of the Law (the "Love Commandments"). How can we place our sermon in the context of modern American life—neighborhood, business, school, or even Church—without reference to the problem of race relations? There is a good parable of this in St. Luke's Gospel. A sophisticated intellectual, well versed in biblical teaching and exegesis, capable of expounding the "Love Commandments" in the abstract, exposed how irrelevant his knowledge was by asking, "But, who is *my neighbor*?" (Luke 10:25-29.) It is all very well to speak of mankind in general, or man in the abstract, but the test comes when we are confronted by *a* man, *a* woman, *a* child, made of flesh and blood! (Or should I say, "covered by skin"?) "To love your neighbor as yourself" means to prove a neighbor to anybody and everybody you come across in your life. In today's world this is impossible without reference to social, cultural, political, and *racial* considerations. Who is my neighbor? What part of the city does he live in? How does he make a living? What are his politics? What is his race? These questions are inescapable.

Race: An Issue for Every Christian

The race crisis is, then, the context in which we preach. Crisis or no crisis, however, the pastor ought to preach on matters pertaining to race relations in the normal course of his ministry. For such a sermon, I personally do not think Race Relations Sunday, or the Sunday in Brotherhood Week, is the most appropriate occasion. Let me draw an analogy. Sermons on race may be compared to sermons on death. Funeral services—or hospital bedsides for that matter—are the last places where sermons on death should be preached. Preaching on death, if it is to do any good, must be done in the normal course of time, to congregations of healthy men, women, and young people. Death, like race, is an inescapable fact of life. The Christian, in order to live a Christian life, must learn how to die a Christian death, and this is not something best learned when death is already upon him. To preach on death, however, is often regarded as something distasteful or morbid, and most pastors seldom do it. We let life insurance salesmen monopolize the business of preparing people for death! In the same way, we pastors have not preached nearly enough (if at all) on the subject of race relations. Yet no one today can escape the question of race in his life any more than he can escape death! Usually, however, we have neglected our obligation to preach about race. The rationalizations are legion: it's too controversial, or it's not biblical, or it's not primarily a spiritual (or moral) issue, and so forth. It is, in fact, all these and more!

In one way or another, sometime or other, everybody, every congregation, every neighborhood, every town and city, is bound to be confronted by the race issue. In fact everybody already is involved in it, whether he lives in an all-white suburban community or in the heart of New York's Harlem. (This is what I mean when I say the race problem constitutes the context in which modern man lives.) It may be in his business, or it may be in the college which his daughter attends, or almost any situation that comes to mind. Indeed, the problem is much closer to him than he may have assumed! There is a sense, therefore, in which everybody today is compelled to come to terms with the issue of race, and yet far too often people do little other than try to postpone "the moment of truth," *as if* by turning away from it they can forever evade facing it. The result is they become so frightened by what they imagine the problem to be, that they resort to violence the moment they can no longer run away from it. Preachers are sometimes criticized for talking about "pie in the sky by and by," but today they could more properly be rebuked for permitting their congregations to remain in a veritable "fool's paradise"!

The Crux of the Race Problem

In terms of the gospel what, then, is the crux of the race problem? From a pastoral point of view, the significant thing is that it has mercilessly revealed the faithlessness of American Christians. The dominant mood of the white community is fear and anxiety, while for the Negro community it is belligerent determination. The reluctance of the white community to change—because of its fear and anxiety—further accentuates the belligerent attitude of the Negro community. This tension, moreover, has in many places reached a point beyond reasonable comprehension. In recent years, especially, communication between the white and the Negro communities has been almost impossible. That is the crux of the race problem for Christians, whether they be white or Negro.

That one Christian cannot fully trust another Christian and be trusted by him for any reason, let alone merely because of difference in race, is intolerable. This is, however, precisely what the present race crisis has come to. *Collectively*, the Negro community has made it clear that it no longer has confidence in the white community or white-dominated institutions, be they government, school, church, industry, trade union, or any other.

Long before the sit-in demonstrations began, Negro leaders in the South, while they trusted some liberal whites, were nevertheless convinced that *they*, the Negro leaders themselves, had to take their *own destiny* in their own hands. The initiative had to be taken by Negro people even though the task could not ultimately be achieved apart from the cooperation of white people. This led to an awareness that the Negro people, if they really wanted to, could do what has been and is required of them in the civil rights struggle. Historically, the successful mass boycott of the Montgomery Bus System in 1955-1956 was a turning point in this respect and, accordingly, is sometimes referred to as the point of emergence of the "new Negro."

In the fall of 1959 the Rev. Ralph Abernathy of Montgomery, Alabama, told me: "Some people say that with the Supreme Court decision of May 17, 1954, communication between the white and Negro communities broke down in the South, but that's not true. There had never been any communication to break down between the two communities before. Only since May, 1954, have we been able to start working to build communication between the two groups. What we are now going through is really a growing pain." The process of building communication between groups that have lost confidence in each other is indeed painful.

An illustration may help to make this point: A decade or so before the 1954 desegregation decision of the Supreme Court, Gunnar Myrdal, in his monumental study *The American Dilemma*, demonstrated, statistically, that what the American Negro wanted most was equality in employment opportunity and what he wanted least was so-called interracial marriage. Most American whites, at the same time, were least unfavorable to according Negroes equal employment opportunities, and most fearful of the prospect of interracial marriage. Such objective testimony, however, has not so far helped to alleviate the fear of miscegenation among the white community, nor has it helped to increase the confidence of the Negro community in the moral integrity of white people. The truth is still that white men do not trust Negroes, and Negroes do not trust white men. This is the fact even though whites and Negroes often say, "Some of my best friends are . . ."

The Christian Vocation: "The Third Race"

There are individuals who trust each other despite the barrier of race. I know a number of such people, and I am sure you, too, know some of them, and I trust that you are one of them. Such individuals are, however, *suspects* in the eyes of the majority, both of their own race and of the other. As such, these exceptional individuals, enjoying one another's confidence within their own *confines*, are unable to do much to build communication between the two races. In a sense they are a "third race," or "marginal race," ostracized by both whites and Negroes. Professing Christians should be prepared to be so ostracized, but they must not be content with their ostracism. (This is a familiar problem of Christians—sometimes called a martyr complex.) The Christian vocation is not to accept ostracism by both races but to reconcile one to the other.

It is for this purpose that Christians have been chosen as a *third race* whose destiny is no other than to be "Suffering Servants" of the Lord, "despised and rejected" by both races and yet "bearing the griefs and carrying the sorrows" of each race (Isa. 42:1-4; 49:1-6; 52:13—53:12). In New Testament terms, they are called to the way of the Cross, to "create . . . one new man in place of the two, that so making peace, they might reconcile *us both* to God in one body through the Cross, thereby bringing the hostility to an end" (Eph. 2:15-16). This is precisely what it means for Christians, in and through the Church, to participate in the divine ministry of reconciliation of man to God and in the redemption of the world. Short of proclaiming this, no sermon can be called Christian preaching, even though it be delivered from the pulpit by a man clad in clerical garb and gifted with the use of biblical language!

The Theology of Race

MANY thoughtful Christians today feel a deep need for a more *theological* treatment of race problems. Whether the term "a theology of race" should be used in this connection may be debatable. It is certain, however, that exclusively sociological and psychological studies of the moral and ethical problems involved in race hostility and ethnic tension are insufficient. Christian theology must also be applied rigorously to this whole question.

The Challenge to Theology

The reasons for this have already been stated. Let us briefly repeat them:

1. Race and ethnic tension is, in a profound sense, a significant part of the social and cultural context within which every Christian today must try to live a Christian life. No Christian can wait for the race problem to go away before trying to be a Christian. He therefore must *accept* (not, however, acquiesce in) the existence of the race crisis, and face it squarely.

2. The problem is basically not a problem of race: that is, the problem does not lie *in* race *per se*, but elsewhere as we have seen. We have only to ask ourselves a few questions to determine this. How should the Christian under-

stand the differences of race which exist among men? Do they belong to the order of creation, or are they accidents of history? Should they arbitrarily keep men apart, or should they have nothing more to do with interpersonal relationships than differences in the color of eyes or hair? Are we talking here about psychological and moral issues, primarily, or about the very nature of man? In other words, are we in the area of anthropology, primarily, or in the area of theology?

The race crisis is, then, at once the social and cultural context in which Christian theology itself needs to be thoroughly re-examined, and a profoundly theological problem in itself. Sociology, psychology, and anthropology clearly have a place in meeting the issues the race crisis has raised, but the fundamental responsibility of theology cannot, for that reason, be ignored.

Some Pertinent Empirical Observations

Two empirical observations can be made at this point that will help to illuminate the nature of the race problem:

1. The race crisis is fundamentally a problem of *intergroup* relations rather than *interpersonal* relations. Between individuals race differences can be overcome relatively easily, but between groups there is much greater difficulty. The fact that individuals can and do transcend differences of race, moreover, frequently becomes a focal point of race tensions in the community at large. The issue of interracial marriage is a case in point. Two persons want to marry because to them the race difference between them is not, or has never been, a problem. Within the total community, however, such a marriage is likely to accentuate existing race tensions. Interracial mariage cannot, for this reason,

be recommended as a method of solving the race problem. It is, furthermore, sacrilegious to use marriage for any purpose other than marriage itself.

2. Race is not so much a biological as a sociological phenomenon. It is not race *per se* that needs to be understood, but *the group*, of which race is often a distinguishing characteristic. There has been in recent years a growing tendency to emphasize the importance of group identification. The development of tribal clubs as voluntary groups in urban Africa in the wake of the breakdown of the tribal community in rural Africa is a conspicuous example of this. Exclusive clubs and associations, Negro and white, in America today are another example.

Experience Affects Theology

Traditional Christian theology conceived of the doctrine of man (anthropology) either in terms of mankind as a whole (the *universal*) or in terms of the individual person (the *particular*). Little attention was paid to the *collective* or social grouping as a mode of existence in history. In preindustrial society Sumner's concept of society as "a group of groups" may have been valid and adequate. In modern industrial society, however, where naturally constituted groups are breaking down, sociologists have found the concept of the "reference group" more useful. In Sumner's concept each individual has his place, and a useful function to perform in his group, which in turn gave him status, a sense of importance, and dignity as a man. In the modern concept, each individual makes his own moral decisions, which shape his personality, in response to the demands made upon him by various groups to which he is related.

Race is one of the unique "reference" groups characteristic of modern societies. It is a convenient symbol of group identification based both on nature and history. This reference to race has come at a time when individuals feel increasingly lost, uprooted from old group structures—for example, kinship group, clan, or tribal community. Faced with a deep need for a group with which to identify himself, contemporary man finds race to be a convenient agent or instrument of group identification.

It follows from this development in history that new thought must be given in theology to the relation between the redemption of the world and the salvation of the individual soul. If the individual finds his identity mainly through membership in several groups, whether naturally structured, historically developed, or both, can his salvation be possible without reference to those groups? Personal salvation traditionally was understood to mean being "chosen" out of all such groups, and redemption of the world was conceived as a cosmic event beyond history. The race crisis in the modern world opens a new dimension of the theology of salvation (soteriology). The redemption of the world can now be seen as an event taking place *in* history, and personal salvation can be seen as an event taking place *within* group experience. There is a real need today for a more articulate doctrine of "redemption of history," and of salvation in a social and cultural context.

The Theological Issue

Thus the issue of race falls within the framework of the doctrine of redemption, not the doctrine of creation. This means that it has to do with the new creation in Christ, not the original creation recorded in *Genesis*. To put it differently, the *Christian* question is not, "Why did God allow different races to develop within the one mankind he created after his own image," but, "What is God doing in history with several different races that have come to be set in conflict with one another?" Acts 17, often cited to justify race segregation (or *apartheid*), has a totally different meaning when read within the framework of redemption. "And he [God] made from one every nation [or race] of men to live on all the face of the earth, having determined allotted periods and the boundaries of their habitation, that they should seek God . . ." (Acts 17:26 f.).

In the context of redemption-history (*Heilsgeschichte*), it is irrelevant which son of Noah's the Negro race might have originated from, and other such questions are equally irrelevant. What matters is what God is doing with the racial and ethnic communities he created. It is to this issue that the race crisis of recent years speaks more eloquently than all biblical exegesis put together! For at long last people of all races, and especially of the Negro race, are accepting themselves for what they are, including their racial identity, despite the handicaps it may involve for them.

Ultimate Questions

The problem is, however, even more profound. Is not the need for group identification as a means of self-assertion in itself a mark of the fallen nature of man? Regeneration, therefore, requires that a man transcend all group identifications, and find fulfillment in Christ, transcending even his own family, as well as his race, tribe, social class, and so on. This, in turn, means that, having been freed from all the groups to which he naturally and/or historically belongs, the Christian becomes free also to relate himself to and enter into communion with everybody and anybody, irrespective of the groups to which they may or may not belong.

Another important point here is that the freedom of the Christian can be realized only within the context of a re-demption of the group or groups to which he belongs. "The courage to be," to use Tillich's phrase, derives from mem-bership in one or several human groups. This fact compels us to re-examine the very nature of the Church, the congre-gation to which we belong. Is it a true community of those who are in Christ, or is it merely another human group through which men assert their identities? This is precisely the question confronting churches today in the American South, especially, and in South Africa.

Finally comes the question: What does it mean to be a Christian in a racially divided society? Whatever it may mean, we know for sure it is neither for the white man simply to be kind and fair to the Negro (willingly to grant him an ever growing share in the "white man's burden") nor for the Negro to be more patient and forgiving toward his oppressors (to be a bigger and better Uncle Tom). It does not mean merely to participate in community actions to reduce race and ethnic tensions, or to work for the elimi-nation of race discrimination in education, employment, housing, and so on. Such actions inevitably follow as fruits or consequences of something much deeper—namely, the acceptance of all people as human persons whose intrinsic value and dignity are equal to one's own in the eyes of God.

The Crux of the Theological Challenge

The most serious challenge to the Church is posed by the large number of "Christians" who find it difficult to accept as their equals people of races other than their own, and to seek acceptance by them as their equals, neither superior nor inferior to each other. There are many churches in the United States which support missionary work in Africa but are opposed to receiving Negroes into their membership. There are churches in South Africa which support the government *apartheid* policy while at the same time vigorously pursuing missionary work among the "natives." Such churches, in both countries, are composed of one race that is predominant, and reflect the prevailing attitude of that race toward other races.

It should also be noted that an increasing number of Negroes would prefer to have nothing to do with members of the now dominant white race. They say, in effect: "We have been subjected to an unbearable degree of humiliation long enough by them. Whatever they may say with their lips, deep down in their hearts they are looking down on us. In the last resort we can no more count on them to make us truly free than on the angelic hosts in heaven. By associating with any of them we shall only be deceiving ourselves. The best thing for us to do is to write off all of them as our enemies, forget them, and start shaping our own destiny with our own hands." So saying, not a small number of Negroes in America and in Africa have turned their back on white people as a whole.

It is tragic that there is such alienation between the dominant and minority groups within one society where the interests and well-being of both are dependent upon reconciliation. It is even more tragic that this condition affects the Church itself. Nothing less is required of the Church than a serious re-examination of its pastoral ministry. What, under these circumstances, is the ultimate meaning of Christian nurture, the ministry of the Word and sacraments, the ministry of fellowship and mutual edification? Can a Christian fulfill his ministry through philanthropy without involving himself in person-to-person fellowship with those toward whom he is beneficent? What should the Church do about such well-intentioned members? Moralistic exhortation on the Christian duty to love one's neighbor as oneself, and scientific explanations of the folly of racism, are not likely to help much. To acquiesce in mistaken views certainly does not help, but this is what the clergy are so often tempted to do. Not infrequently, it is unfortunately necessary to add, the clergy themselves share the racist views prevailing in their flocks.

Many questions have been raised, and there are no easy answers for any of them. Pat answers are no answers at all, and are, in fact, worse than no answers. Much ecumenical study will be necessary in the realm of theology proper and in social ethics, before adequate answers to these questions can be expected.

One point strongly demands reiteration: The race crisis is a serious challenge to the Church because it is a problem for many members of the Church. I am not unmindful of the vicious hate-mongers, crackpots, and authentic racists, or of the political forces that are trying to make capital out of the race prejudices of others. If the problem only involved such people, ways to solve it could have been found long ago.

The crux of the matter is how to address mostly decent people, and especially those within the Church, who somehow cannot see the human person beneath the skin if the color of that skin is different from their own. Yet the culprit is not the color of the other person's skin, but the historically conditioned outlook of the viewer.

Contemporary race and ethnic tension constitutes the social and cultural context within which theological thinking is sharply challenged. By the same token, rapid social change in Africa and Asia under the impact of Western civilization for the past century and a half constitutes a historical context within which modern man is challenged to analyze, reassess and finally reformulate his outlook on race.

The Meaning of the Global Race Revolution

Race has, historically, been a source of human pride and human shame—both unwarranted and undeserved—and has hindered men from entering into creative relationships one with another. Race pride has "colored" much of the missionary enterprise and philanthropic work carried on by the white race among other races, often with paternalism and often with authoritarianism, and always grounded in condescension: helping the weak, civilizing the primitive, developing the underdeveloped, or "giving" to the poor. It is, however, because of the missionary and philanthropic enterprises which accompanied white colonial imperialism that we now observe a global race revolution. Race pride in the white man has made it a tacit condition that unless others become like him, they are not fully civilized and cannot claim equality with him. Yet, what the white man has done *to* and *for* other races throughout the world has helped them to acquire self-respect as members of the human "race."

At this stage of history those born members of the Caucasian (white) race inherit undeserved advantages and privileges, and those born members of other races inherit disadvantages and handicaps. Race relations have largely meant how privileged white people should help under-privileged "colored" people. Members of the "colored" races have been encouraged to become like white people (to be accepted by white people as "one of them"), and white people have *enjoyed* helping "colored" people become "white." To accept people of other races *and to seek their acceptance* has seldom occurred among white people.

All this is, however, changing in the present race revolution. Today no self-respecting Negro seeks to "pass" as a white man in order to be accepted in a "white man's world." He demands that he be treated as a human being, a first-class citizen, neither in spite of nor because of, but notwithstanding his being a Negro. He accepts himself as God has made him to be, including his "negritude," and he demands of others that they accept him as he is, including his "negritude." What is happening (and it makes this the most exciting age in the history of race relations) is that the white man is accepting himself as he is, with all his built-in privileges and advantages, not in pride (as if he had acquired them by his own efforts) but in humility and in repentance ("Lord, I am not worthy"). At the same time, the Negro is accepting himself as he is, with all his built-in handicaps and disadvantages, not with a chip on his shoulder, not in passive resignation or self-pity, but with a renewed sense of vocation as one God has chastised to test and purify his inner strength. In this sense, it is possible to speak of a "vocation of a race," or a "vocation of a nation," or even a "vocation of a generation." All of this takes place, moreover, in the context of the *history of salvation!*

This is the good news inherent in the contemporary race crisis which needs to be proclaimed from every pulpit of the Church—consistently, boldly, emphatically, and triumphantly.

PART III

Pastoral
Counseling

Pastoral Counseling
on the Race Issue

THERE are, of course, obvious problems confronting the pastoral counselor: how to persuade a racially prejudiced parishioner to stay in a congregation which is about to become multiracial; how to calm the mother whose daughter seems determined to marry a man of a different race; how to counsel an urban vestry and congregation whether to flee to a suburb or to stay downtown and become a racially inclusive Church. The problems, however, that will concern us here lie at a much deeper level (and are much more subtle in nature).

Counseling as Therapy

It may be well, first of all, to make clear what I mean by counseling, or what might be called the "therapeutic ministry." I believe the emphasis in counseling should be healing, not correction; recovery, not reform. We ought to be concerned centrally about the health of the counselee as a person, as a free moral agent. Is he a healthy man, a total human being, a whole personality? If not, how can he be helped to become one? This is what the counseling ministry is all about, and obviously it cannot be conducted apart from, or short of, sustained interaction (interpersonal dialogue) between the counselor and the counselee.

Jesus said, "Those who are well have no need of a physician, but those who are sick" (Matt. 9:12). What, however, is the need of those who are sick but do not know they are? Sent into the world by Christ himself to carry out his own ministry, we pastors are to "heal the sick, raise the dead, cleanse lepers, cast out demons" (Matt. 10:8). Surely this is true whether or not the sick are aware of their sickness. The ministry of counseling often has to begin by calling to the attention of the sick that they *are* sick.

The term "sickness" may be too strong a word—"problem" or "predicament" may be less objectionable. Whatever word we use, our attention will be focused on three points: *man, society*, and the *interaction* between the two. To put it in general terms, there is something wrong—and not only in a strictly moral sense—there is something wrong with modern man, with our society, and with the relationship between them. The race crisis which is upon us today is at once the symptom, the evidence, and the substance of what has gone wrong in our time.

The Prejudiced Person: A Working Definition

I am not saying that race prejudice is a mental illness, or that anyone who harbors race prejudice ought to see a psychiatrist. I do say that race prejudice is not primarily a moral choice freely made by an individual and, therefore, to be judged bad, wrong, or unjust; it is, rather, one expression of the total personality of the person. This is why those who are prejudiced do not know there is anything wrong with them. Telling them how wrong they are will do no good at all.

Rarely, if ever, has a prejudiced person approached his pastor seeking counsel about his prejudice! It is more accurate to say "he is prejudiced" than "he has a prejudice." Prejudice is a serious problem when it has become built into a total personality structure. Everybody has (possesses) all sorts of prejudices. The fallen nature of man as creature makes this inevitable. Only a man profoundly prejudiced *for* himself would seriously claim he has no prejudice whatsoever. ("I used to be conceited, but not any more. Now I'm perfect.") Anyone who says he has no prejudice is a fool or a liar. But there is a great difference between *having* prejudices and *being* prejudiced. *To be prejudiced* is *to have a prejudice* so *ingrained* that it has become, in effect, a sort of *second nature*.

The Initiative Rests with the Pastor

One difficulty, then, in counseling with reference to race relations is that those who really need counseling rarely know it and seldom find their way to a pastor's study on their own initiative. The initiative has to be taken by the pastor. But, obviously, he cannot easily spot "problem people" in his congregation and zero in on them, nor can he assume that everybody is a problem. Neither can a conscientious pastor wait for something to happen (Mrs. X of the congregation is asked to rent a room to a Negro student; it is rumored a Negro family is moving in next door to the Y family; etc.). It is no use waiting for something to happen that will expose those who are problems and those who are not (separate the goats from the sheep), for by then it will be too late to do much good. Where should the pastor begin?

The Pastor Should Begin with Himself

Before he can become a psychoanalyst a man must be psychoanalyzed himself. Before we pastors attempt to counsel others on race matters, we should subject ourselves to some therapeutic self-analysis. Problems of race relations afflict the vast majority of people in our society, including ministers.

This indeed is the crux of the matter: None of us knows confidently who he is in relation to his neighbors in the context of a commonly shared world. That is why, basically, we continue to have "race problems" despite phenomenal advances in the biological, social, and behavioral sciences in recent decades, and despite ancient moral imperatives common to all world religions. Conversely, our inability to respond adequately to the race crisis reveals how we have lost, or not yet gained, our true identities within society, as members of the human community intended by God.

Every pastor, then, must first of all examine himself in relation to these problems.

The Ultimate Aim of Counseling

Counseling on race relations does not mean to advise a Negro Christian to maintain confidence in white people (to be patient), or to advise a white Christian not to sell his house because the house next door has been sold to a Negro family (to be tolerant). Christian counseling aims to help each person to find and be true to himself, to be the person God wants him to be, in relation to his neighbors, old and new, far and near, present and prospective. Today in the

United States "neighbors" necessarily include people of several different racial and ethnic backgrounds.

A person may be able to avoid living with someone he dislikes, but he will have to live with himself, no matter what and all the time. Counseling on race relations, therefore, can most appropriately begin by asking such questions as: What are current race tensions doing to us and to our neighbors? Why do we (as whites) react the way we do to the emergence of the "new Negro" and his demands? Why do we (as Negroes) do what we are doing, say what we are saying, act as we are acting, *today*, when we did not, say, five years ago?

The First Step

It is important that the questions be asked in the *first person plural*, because the problem of race is, in the final analysis, a problem for all of us. We are all equally involved, not in isolation one from another but all together. No effective therapy is possible so long as the problem is looked upon as belonging to others: to integrationists or to segregationists; to white people or to Negro people; to progressives or to moderates; and so forth.

The basic prerequisite for effective therapy is, then, to accept the fact that we are all involved (whether we choose to be or not) in the race crisis, and *that each of us has to bear responsibility for its resolution just as we share responsibility for its existence.*

And when we say *all* of us are responsible that means not only the prejudiced people we seek to counsel but pastors and would-be counselors just as much.

Group Counseling

Such being the case, counseling on race relations can often be done effectively in a group situation, where each member of the group is helped to look at himself *within* a racial context. Such therapy is radically different from introspective self-examination, or from an analysis by a specialist. Given the widespread and deep-seated bad conscience (or at the least, uneasy conscience) with respect to race problems, neither of these methods of private therapy is likely to prove helpful. The first tends *either* to rationalization *or* to morbid self-mortification (remorsefulness). The latter tends to evoke resistance to the suggestions of the specialist. Somehow or other a therapeutic group (community) needs to be brought into being in order to make counseling on race relations really effective.

The pastor's role in group counseling is different from that of a father-confessor who hears the confession of an individual and gives him advice and absolution. He must be the pivotal point of a therapeutic community in which everybody (pastor included) is a counselor and a counselee to everybody else! Ideally, every Christian congregation ought to be such a community, but the plain fact is that few of them actually are or are likely to be. Most pastors will find they must begin by forming one or more smaller groups within the congregation.

Objectives of the Counseling Ministry

What should the counseling ministry seek to achieve in the area of race relations? Through counseling we strive to gain insight into the true nature of the race crisis as well as into our own true natures. A number of considerations need specific discussion because they affect one or both of the basic objectives.

1. SEPARATION OF THE NEGRO AND WHITE COMMUNITIES. Every one of us, regardless of his stand on segregation versus integration, must strive to understand that in America, despite the Constitution, civil rights legislation, and Supreme Court decisions on race issues, the white and the Negro communities are by and large living in two separate worlds.* These worlds are separated by such obvious differences as per-capita income, percentage of college graduates, rate of chronic or structural unemployment, infant mortality, and many, many other economic and social criteria.

Of much greater importance is the social and psychological dynamics which keep the two communities apart, one from the other. Negroes are united by an aspiration for things yet to be achieved, while whites are united by a concern for things they have already achieved and now fear to lose. The Negro group tends to be future-oriented, while the white group, more or less, tends to be past-oriented. For this reason, the average white man, without considerable effort, cannot appreciate the full meaning of the grievances or the aspirations of the "new Negro." This difficulty has been made virtually insurmountable by the

* I am mindful that some will perhaps criticize my using the term "community" in this context, and I would like to say that I use the term advisedly. There is a sense in which all people known as Negro share in a common plight in American society today *vis-à-vis* white people, or in the face of the white-dominated mores, and thus are *forced* to be united one with another at least on this basis. Likewise, the rise of the so-called "new Negro" is bound to affect the life of all white people regardless of their personal outlooks. For this and a number of other reasons it is not unreasonable to use the terms "Negro" and "white" communities.

century-long pattern of social segregation, whether *de facto* segregation in the North or legalized (*de jure*) segregation in the South. The first thing white people must learn is that to appreciate what the "new Negro" is talking about, dispassionate, unhurried face-to-face confrontations and conversations are indispensable. The Negro people, for their part, must realize how nearly impossible it is for the average white man to appreciate what they are complaining about and aspiring for. For such understanding, Christian sympathy and magnanimity are required, which, *humanly speaking*, is perhaps too much to expect of Negro people in the present situation.

2. RAPID SOCIAL CHANGE AND THE PROBLEM OF ADJUSTMENT. It is not primarily race differences as such that disturb the ordinary man, but the thought that he might have to associate with people who are total strangers. This applies equally to political, industrial, financial, and even (perhaps especially) religious institutions. In such a society as ours it is futile and wasteful to try to keep one group of people apart from another on any such basis as race, ethnic origin, or religion. It would make as much sense to separate them on the basis of color of eyes or hair.

America in 1964 is a radically different society from America in 1864 (or even 1934). Industrial and technological advances have brought about a *metropolitan culture* in which the population is highly mobile, and the smaller community is increasingly pluralistic and multiracial. In such a society no power structure can long remain vital unless it is *centralized and decentralized simultaneously*.

Such a society is plausible when we are reading about it in books, but in reality to most of us it is a disturbing and uncomfortable environment in which to live. The Israelites wandering in the wilderness, having lost their direction to the promised land, longingly looked back to the false security of Egyptian bondage. Modern Americans, bewildered by an increasingly dynamic, open, and pluralistic society, longingly look back to what they imagine was once a cozy, comfortable, and closed community.

Race separation is a *device* used by men lost and confused in the *wilderness of an impersonal industrial society* to create a temporary oasis, an arbitrarily closed community.

3. CONFUSION OF STANDARDS. The rapid and radical change that American society *as a whole* is undergoing has created confusion about standards for making ethical decisions. Injunctions that have for centuries been accepted without question are now challenged. For example, "Love thy neighbor as thyself." In a pre-industrial, closed community it was not difficult to know one's neighbors (though it was probably difficult to love them). In modern society we often do not even know who our neighbors are. Proximity of residence does not necessarily make people neighbors any more. Human relationships, moreover, are fragmented in all sorts of ways: notably, the tendency to have different places to live in, to work in, to play in, to shop in, to go to school in, and so forth. It is difficult indeed to love a neighbor when one does not even know who he is! Erich Fromm puts it this way: ". . . modern man feels uneasy and more and more bewildered. . . . While his power over nature grows, he feels powerless in his individual life and in society. . . ." *

* Erich Fromm, *Man for Himself: An Inquiry into the Psychology of Ethics* (New York: Holt, Rinehart & Winston, 1947), p. 4.

It is the same lonely situation that makes a man *crave* a cozy, closed circle of people to whom he can be related without pretense or disguise and in whose presence he can be his natural self. In our industrial culture, however, such a group is not found among fellow workers because they are usually competitors and rivals. Most people lead extremely lonely lives today. This is one reason why we have a strong trend toward conformism in contemporary American society.

One powerful manifestation of this conformity is the prevalence of race prejudice and discrimination. Under the strong fear of miscegenation we can discern vestiges of tribalism, and the individual's deep need to perpetuate an in-group which gives him self-identity.

4. ROOTLESSNESS AND RACISM. We begin to perceive the basic reason why, despite the exhorting of the Church, the teaching of the schools, and the legislating of the government, race tensions remain acute among us. Ours is a society in which many have lost a sense of identity and are suffering from intense insecurity and lostness. An insecure, lost person is incapable of loving anybody, including himself. This is the root of the problems of race (and other human) relations in our society.

Let us take another look at the lack of communication between the Negro and white communities. In the light of the prevalent insecurity, it would have been astonishing if the white community had accepted desegregation without resistance. For many white people a racially exclusive society is the last opportunity for a closed society with privileges, prestige, and other symbols of status. For the same reason, a racially exclusive society is regarded by most Negro people as a reminder of humiliation dating back to the days of slavery, and therefore an evil to be eradicated at once.

If these observations are valid it logically follows that desegregation of local churches will not take place until long after the desegregation of schools and residential areas has been achieved.

How difficult it is to make responsible decisions on matters that involve race problems. The moral issue involved would seem to be clear. How, then, can men of intelligence and good will make such preposterous decisions? How, for example, can the possible depreciation of property value if owned or rented by a Negro family seriously affect the judgment of apparently intelligent people? How can Christians, of all people, choose to "save their skins" at the expense of their souls, or elect to protect property values to the disregard of human values?

The answers do not rest in any lack of sound biological and sociological information on race. Nor can we find answers in some extreme viciousness or overabundance of ill will in society. The answers are found in the lack of generally accepted, objective standards by which to make decisions on problems involving race relations.

Prejudice, then, is a crutch; especially when it is based on race, it becomes a tangible device insecure people can employ to exclude a certain group of people from the category of neighbors. It does not help establish which neighbors we *are* to love, but it does establish which neighbors we *need* not love! The logic of prejudice, furthermore, adds one group after another to the list of those to be categorically excluded. Eventually, of course, the number of neighbors a man has is reduced to that of the man and "his kind."

Conclusion

These are the considerations we pastors need to explore with our congregations, especially when we are exercising our function to counsel. Whether we counsel individuals or groups (or the congregation as a whole) will depend, of course, upon the circumstances, and also upon the particular gifts we happen to possess. The objective always is nothing less than to help reconcile the individual Christian to himself, first of all, and then to the congregation, and, finally, through the congregation to the whole world—to each and every other man.

6

The Theological Bases
of Counseling

PREJUDICE is essentially an evasion of ethical decisions. It is a subjective method of escaping from the cold facts of real life—a flight into a world of fantasy! The effect of prejudice is to create a fool's paradise in which one lives and behaves *as if* certain people do not exist, by virtue of the fact that one has categorically eliminated them ("out of mind, out of sight"). Such a fantasy places a person under irreconcilable tensions between reality and fantasy, and these tensions drive him further and further from reality into fantasy!

Prejudice: A Technique of Evasion

The person becomes a *prejudiced personality*—not merely a person who has prejudices. He becomes, in a very real sense, a *warped personality*. Dr. Erich Fromm's words are to the point:

. . . problems of ethics cannot be omitted from the study of personality, either theoretically or therapeutically. The value judgments we make determine our actions, and upon their validity rests our mental health and happiness. . . . Neurosis itself is, in the last analysis, a symptom of moral failure (although "adjustment" is by no means a symptom of moral achievement).

And significantly Dr. Fromm goes on to say:

In many instances a neurotic symptom is the specific expression of moral conflict, and the success of . . . [a] therapeutic effort depends on the understanding and solution of the person's moral problem.*

Counseling on race relations must, obviously, help people in general to face up to reality and, in particular, help those who are trying to run away from reality. How can it be done most effectively?

A person who has taken flight into fantasy to solve imagined problems becomes a problem himself. He becomes, in fact, *the* problem. He cannot be helped by rational argument, because he is, in point of fact, irrational.

I am reminded of the story of a woman who convinced herself she was dead. She went to her doctor and announced that she was dead, and demanded that he write a death certificate for her. No argument would persuade her that she was still alive. Finally, the doctor said: "Madam, do you think a dead person bleeds?" She answered, "No, doctor, I don't believe so." Thereupon, the doctor took a needle and punched a hole in one of her fingers. Blood came out. "Look here, Madam," began the doctor, but before he could say more, the woman said, "Oh, I now see that a dead person does bleed."

When a *group* of people fall into this kind of fantasy the problem becomes much more complicated. So long as we

* Fromm, *Man for Himself: An Inquiry into the Psychology of Ethics* (New York: Holt, Rinehart & Winston, 1947), p. viii.

try to confront what *they claim* the problems are, we cannot begin to help them. Talking to them directly *about themselves* will not do, because they cannot be objective about themselves. Their need is to look at themselves in perspective so they can see that *they* are the problem. It is rare that we can approach a person as Nathan approached David—confronting him directly and declaring, "You are the man"—and get a result as favorable as Nathan did. To tell such people that they are the problem will, in nine cases out of ten, result in alienating them or even convincing them that there is something wrong with the counselor. That is why I have argued that group therapy is a more effective approach.

Understanding Prejudice

It is imperative, if we are to counsel intelligently, that we understand why white people do not, or cannot, *hear* what Negro Americans are saying clearly and emphatically. To be sure, there have been in recent years, and there will continue to be for some long time to come, many repugnant incidents—vandalism and violence, riots and bloodshed—on the part of Negro people. It is not suggested that such antisocial behavior is to be condoned, but neither should such incidents be used as reasons to deny Negro Americans equality. This violence is more than balanced by the antisocial behavior of some white Americans against Negroes, such as the bombing of many churches, the murder of innocent children and civil rights leaders.

We pastors will be ill-advised to become judgmental when confronted by violence in either the white or the Negro communities. It will be more helpful if we seek to gain insights into the reasons for the violence. Unfortunately, many clergymen seem incapable of seeing beneath the violence the causes which produce it.

To reach such understanding requires a warm heart and a cool head and some plain hard work. Negro Americans and white Americans have lived in two different worlds, albeit in the same country. To the white American the world of the Negro is no less strange than Zanzibar, and the tensions between white and Negro Americans are more acute than those between the United States and Zanzibar because in the United States the two share exactly a common geographical area and use the same language! (I am reminded of the famous dictum of George Bernard Shaw: "Great Britain and the United States are two countries divided by one language.") John Howard Griffin, who dared, at the risk of his life, darken his skin to discover at first hand what it is like to be a Negro in the American South, put it this way:

How else except by becoming a Negro could a white man hope to learn the truth? Though we lived side by side throughout the South, communication between the two races had simply ceased to exist. Neither really knew what went on with those of the other race.*

Speaking as an American Negro, James Baldwin has said:

I had tried . . . to convey something of what it felt like to be a Negro and no one had been able to listen. . . . And . . . the really ghastly thing about trying to convey to a white man the reality of the Negro experience has nothing whatever to do with the fact of color, but has to do with

* John Howard Griffin, *Black Like Me* (New York: New American Library—Signet Books), p. 7.

this man's relationship to his own life. He will face in your life only what he is willing to face in his.*

Man, regardless of his race, color, creed, or culture, tends to build a private world of his own, withdraw into it, and stay in it as long as possible. This is what a sense of security comes to mean. The private world of one who belongs to a minority group is constantly affected by what happens in the world of the dominant group. For that reason, members of minority groups are sensitive to what members of the dominant group think, say, and do. On the other hand, the private world of one who belongs to a dominant group is largely unaffected by what happens within the minority groups, and members of a dominant group tend to be indifferent to what is going on within minority groups. Inevitably, this difference in mental attitude widens the chasm between the two worlds, making communication between them all the more difficult.

Ultimately, both sides must leave behind their private worlds, which are only illusions anyway, and face the fact that they share one and the same world, whether they like it or not. For this experience members of minority groups are much better prepared than those of a privileged dominant group. Negro Americans are already addressing themselves to the real problem, namely, the attainment of civil and human rights for *all* citizens, freedom and dignity for *all* people, and self-respect for *all* persons in a fulfilled democracy. They have painfully learned that so long as there continue to be persons who

* James Baldwin, *Nobody Knows My Name* (New York: Dial), p. 221.

are denied their rights, the rights of all are threatened.

This insight is, however, difficult for most white Americans to accept for several reasons. In the first place, white people have been so *protected* (insulated) in their prestige and privilege as members of a dominant group, that they cannot appreciate the depth and scope of indignity and humiliation suffered by Negro Americans entirely on account of their race. In the second place, they mostly believe they have never consciously oppressed members of Negro or any other ethnic group. They may have done nothing *for* them, but in their own minds they have never done anything against them. It is not surprising, therefore, that they do not consider race prejudice a moral issue.

In the third place, it is emotionally repugnant to them that the evils of racism are being exposed by Negro citizens. To admit the validity of what is being said by Negro citizens is deemed to be the same as *giving in* to their demands, and is, therefore, a *defeat* for the white race. (This, of course, is not the case objectively but is felt to be so emotionally.)

Finally, many white Americans feel that to accord Negro Americans first-class citizenship will somehow cost white citizens privileges which heretofore they have enjoyed exclusively. In fact, they will lose none of the privileges except exclusiveness. Yet to those to whom racial exclusiveness is something of the ultimate mark of distinction, prestige and privilege, this of course is deemed to be a tragedy, but mankind as a whole can ill afford to continue allowing such people to stay in their own private paradise much longer.

The Ministry of Counseling and Prejudice

Race is the context in which we witness to the gospel, and an ethical issue to which the gospel is addressed. To single out race, however, and treat it as if it were the root of all evils is a pathological preoccupation, and as such, is precisely the sickness or predicament from which contemporary man must be freed. It is all too easy to "deliver them to Satan" (1 Tim. 1:20), that is, to declare that they are not Christian, to excommunicate them, to label them as segregationists, racists, and so forth. What is required is that we help them to face reality.

Many pastors are tempted to say, "They are basically sincere Christians despite their race prejudice. They are inflexible on this one issue, but otherwise are perfectly good Christians." This can be supported by citing episodes out of their lives to prove how kindly disposed or generous they are toward Negro servants, foreign students, and so forth. Far too often pastors have done just this, thereby permitting "otherwise sincere and kindhearted" Christians to continue living in a fool's paradise at the expense of justice in our society, not to mention the human and civil rights of such fellow citizens as happen to belong to the "wrong" race or ethnic group!

Counseling on race relations is essentially different from *advice-giving* on how to treat members of other races, or *moral exhortation* to the effect that one must respect people regardless of race, or the imparting of *scientific information* intended to enlighten people about the nature of race. We must strive to help people who are anxious and fearful, living amidst acute race tensions, face up to what, under God, is actually happening, and what God, in the race crisis, is demanding of them.

Christians gathering in the presence of God, in humility and determination, "with the Bible in one hand and the daily press in the other," should aim not to solve race problems as such, but to discover what God wills each of them to do in reference to the race crisis. Such a gathering of Christians is a therapeutic community and is needed in every congregation. If it can be developed on an ecumenical, multiracial, transcongregational basis it will be so much the more effective.

This is the challenge to the ministry of counseling. Every pastor, and the congregation committed to his charge, must face it squarely if they are to live contemporaneously with the mighty act of God in history. Any fantasy, including the fantasy of racism, is an evasion of the will of God, and the way out of fantasy is to permit God's will to operate among us.

The Task of the Church

In this context the task of the Church, especially in the ministry of counseling, is manifold:

1. To interpret, in light of biblical revelation and Christian theology, the mighty act of God working through contemporary social change toward an emerging world society.

2. To help create opportunities for members of minority and dominant groups to engage one another in person-to-person dialogue on a continuing basis, including the sharing of common burdens. It is only in face-to-face conversation and cooperative involvement that members of different races can finally encounter one another as persons

and hear one another without distortion or misunderstanding. Such encounters will not naturally or automatically take place because of civil rights legislation, but will, on the contrary, be resisted by those who are convinced that they have got along perfectly well all by themselves in the past and can continue to do so in the future.

3. To help people in general, and the congregation in particular, to know what the Civil Rights Act of 1964 and comparable state and local legislation does *not* say as well as what it *does* say. There is much misunderstanding based on ignorance or willful misrepresentation so that civil rights legislation is widely misconstrued. Laws are tools which require intelligent use in order to do any good. Besides lawmakers (the legislature) and law-enforcement agencies (the police force) there must be law-abiding citizens if democracy is to prevail. This requires understanding by citizens of the meaning of legislation duly enacted.

These tasks are at the core of the ministry of counseling which the Church is called upon to perform in the area of race relations. A comprehensive program, on a sustaining basis, involving skills, insights, and resources available in many professional disciplines, must be recruited.

This is no marginal problem confronting the Church. It is central to the ministry of Christ in the world today. For that reason, we need to direct all our resources, every skill and talent we possess, to bring to our congregations and our communities enlightenment, intelligent counsel and, above all, compassion and wisdom. The greatest of all our resources—the gospel itself—must be brought to bear upon the problem, directly and specifically, enthusiastically and relentlessly.

PART IV

The Pastor and Christian Action

7

Christian Action

on the Race Issue

IN preceding chapters dealing with the background of the race crisis, and with the pastor's role as preacher and counselor in reference to race relations, we have attempted an analysis and appraisal of the race crisis itself. This constitutes a broad background for a discussion of the action a pastor should consider in the area of race relations.

The Church and Other Community Agencies

When we talk about the pastor and the church he represents, we should also think of them in relation to (*a*) government, both as a law-making and a law-enforcing agency; (*b*) public service agencies, governmental and voluntary, which are directly concerned with race problems; (*c*) various social action groups, racial and interracial, including professional human relations agencies; and (*d*) university and other research agencies such as those sponsored by foundations. The pastor and members of the congregation committed to his charge are all, as citizens, more than likely taking part, or ought to be taking part, in some or all of these community activities. Of such activities, however, we shall have little to say except to make occasional reference to them when relevant. We shall concentrate on the actions which are uniquely appropriate for the pastor and the church he represents. Such activities should never be a duplication of, or a poor substitute for, what other agencies are doing or can do.

In considering what action to take, the pastor should think of his action and that of the church he represents in relation to what other agencies are doing and what they are achieving by their various activities. That is to say, the Church as the Church must not act *in isolation* any more than it should duplicate what other agencies are doing. By virtue of its nature the race crisis requires concerted action among as many different academic and professional disciplines as are available, involving people, both experts and laymen, of varied points of view. For this reason, our discussion will touch upon the role of a pastor in community-wide action as well as the action which is specifically appropriate to the Church.

Difference in Needs according to Local Situation

Discussion on action is not easy to conduct in general terms, because each local situation is, of course, different. Some pastors live in large metropolitan areas where there are many churches of the same denomination; where many Christian denominations are well represented; where there are a number of so-called "Negro parishes," and even more all-white churches; where many churches are struggling in changing neighborhoods, some inclined to take flight into suburbia and some making gallant efforts to remain (which means, in most cases, becoming racially and otherwise inclusive churches); where there are all kinds of agencies, organizations, and committees—secular, interfaith, interdenominational, public, private, and what have you. Other pastors live in small towns or villages where there is only one Christian church; where population is declining; and where prospects for new industries are poor. Still other pastors live in middle-sized communities which are, in a sense, "overchurched," either in terms of several denominations competing with one another, or in terms of several churches originally organized along ethnic or cultural lines. In many towns, especially in rural communities, there may be no civic agency, religious or secular, public or private, to be counted as an ally of the Church, except possibly a local school. There are also, of course, towns where the local population is exclusively, or almost exclusively, of one race or ethnic composition. Discussion on action in the area of race relations meaningful to all these situations is not easy to achieve.

Action and Study

During six years of service on the staff of the World Council of Churches I learned two things which are pertinent here: (1) How inseparably linked action and study must be. Action preceded by no study is often misguided, while study followed by no action is obviously fruitless. One might say that study and action must be "integrated" one with the other. (2) Both study and action must be conceived in as wide a perspective as possible and be executed in the given locality as much as possible by local people. For example, ecumenical studies not locally rooted or local actions completely isolated from the "outside" world are equally irrelevant to the Church universal and to the local Christian community. Our discussion of appropriate action on race relations presupposes the discussion in preceding chapters and has its roots in them. An analytical comprehension of the problem involved is essential if any action is to be relevant.

The Local Situation and
the Universal Predicament

Constructive action in the area of race relations must, of course, be tailored to meet local needs, but at the same time it must be remembered that a local community is not, has never been, and never will be an isolated island, and therefore so-called local needs are not necessarily confined to what happens within a given community. The local situation must be viewed and reviewed in a much wider perspective.

In 1962 I made a study of race tensions in Great Britain. One thing was very clear to me as an outsider and yet somehow remained hidden to the eyes of the "natives" (Englishmen in England): Since the end of World War II India, Pakistan, the former British colonies or protectorates in Africa, and especially the West Indies have become as much an economic labor pool of metropolitan England as Northern Ireland had been for many centuries. There are two reasons for this. (1) The West Indies with limited employment opportunities can no longer support its exploding population. (2) Many public services in London and the midlands, including health services and the transport system, would have to be seriously curtailed were it not for the manpower supplied from the West Indies. For this reason, friction between West Indians and Englishmen in England has risen sharply until it has become as great as friction between Irishmen and Englishmen. The problem is how to deal with the situation. Any action to reduce or eliminate interracial tensions between English people and West Indian people is bound to fail unless the effort at the local level takes account of the total situation. For example, efforts to curb immigration are completely unrealistic in face of what one observer has called the phenomenon of "the empire coming home." The tensions are local, but the problem is international.

Another illustration: In 1960 the University College of Salisbury, Southern Rhodesia (then officially called University College of Rhodesia and Nyasaland) was opened on a "desegregated" basis. This was a historic development in Southern Rhodesia. The University College was an institution of the then Federation of Rhodesia and Nyasaland, and for that reason the land on which the university was located was exempt from the law of the Colony of Southern Rhodesia, in which *de facto* segregation was as rigidly enforced as *apartheid* in South Africa. The reaction was predictable. Many colonists in British Central Africa were horrified at the prospect of their sons and daughters attending a multiracial university. Some of them took the trouble to send their children to British universities, where the odds were they would actually be fellow students of a larger number of African students, and certainly would have much freer association with whatever African students were present! The joke, then, was on white parents who tried to protect their children from what they thought was undesirable association with Africans. Action that appeared appropriate from the local point of view brought about the opposite of what was intended. Today, action conceived in terms of nineteenth-century patterns is not only ineffective, but may boomerang!

Action Must Be Prophetic

These illustrations suggest that we should consider possible action not only in terms of *protection* of what is precious to us, or *prevention* of what we fear may be undesirable for us, but more positively in terms of *creating* something new or *promoting* something heretofore untried. Our action must, in other words, be inspired by prophetic insight as well as being based upon careful study of all factors involved. Where we are going cannot be known without knowing where we are and where we have been. At the same time, we cannot clearly understand where we have been and where we are except in terms of where we are heading.

Action under Compulsion

Pent-up resentment and intensified bad conscience frequently drive men to rush into action which may contribute more to the release of emotion than to the solution of a problem. We pastors have to be careful that we ourselves do not act out of such compulsion, since as members of a particular race, we cannot help sharing the resentment and bad conscience *collectively held* by our race. We also have to take into account the fact that many people, including members of the Church, are likely to act under compulsion when confronted with the race crisis. Any incident, or even rumors of an incident, may lead apparently rational people to act hastily. When a number of people are thrown together in common action charged with emotion the situation can easily get out of control. This is another reason why action should be preceded by and based upon study. One of the pastor's responsibilities, it seems to me, is to prevent action under compulsion, whether by individuals or groups, and to this end the ministry of counseling should be exercised.

Action Specifically for the Pastor and the Church

What actions in the area of race relations are uniquely appropriate for the pastor? We shall consider this question under several headings: (1) In reference to the congregation; (2) in reference to the community; and (3) in reference to professional colleagues: pastors of other churches in the community, and fellow pastors within a denominational structure.

Action and the Congregation

It is safe to assume, in nine cases out of ten, that the congregation is predominantly or exclusively of one race, and that within that race are many shades of opinion about race problems, although one position may reflect the sentiments of most members of the congregation. What kind of action is appropriate in such situations, and how should the pastor get things moving?

EXISTING AND FELT NEEDS. The guiding principle is, of course, that existing needs determine the action. Here it is important to distinguish between *existing needs* and *felt needs*. It is not enough to consider what counsel individual members of the congregation may need (felt needs). It is necessary to consider what the congregation as church needs to be in the community (existing needs). This requires intimate and thorough knowledge of the congregation and its position in the community. For example, if the congregation is made up of leading citizens in the community, whether in politics, industry, or civic activities, then as a church the congregation has special obligations—that is, it has a leadership role thrust upon it whether it likes it or not. To disregard this, and to limit counseling to felt needs of different members of the congregation would be a serious mistake on the part of the pastor.

THE CONGREGATION AS AN INTEGRATING COMMUNITY. Action in reference to the congregation should be directed toward making it an *integrating* community, before it can be expected to become a racially integrated congregation. Many white congregations aspire to become racially inclusive but conceive of integration in their own terms, which usually amounts to saying, "Negroes or others who are, or may become, like us are welcome." More generally speaking, white people conceive of integration as a process in which other races or ethnic groups lose their former identities and become *absorbed* into white institutions and groups.

Many pastors in London assured me that the reason West Indian people did not feel welcome in their churches was not because of discrimination, but was, rather, a reflection of the coldness Londoners display to other people in general. That is precisely the point. And, the same problem exists in very many American churches. Unless a congregation has within it a *dynamism* which causes every stranger who enters into its midst to feel wanted, it is useless to try to "desegregate" it by contrived devices. This problem has little to do with the attitude of the congregation toward race as such, or the official position of the Church on race issues. It raises a profound question more fundamental to the spiritual health of the congregation: Is the congregation composed of "apostles" sent out into the world, or is it a club of dues-paying members? If it is the latter, even if it should become racially integrated, it would probably be as stuffy and exclusive as any other exclusive club. It would be made up entirely of "our kind" of people regardless of race or color. This might be an "integrated" community, but it is certainly not an *integrating* community.

PATHOLOGICAL PREOCCUPATION WITH THE RACE CRISIS. One important action of a pastor on race relations may very well be to turn the mind of the congregation away from preoccupation with race problems as such, and renew its sense of mission to the world. This the pastor can do through his preaching, teaching, and counseling, and in all aspects of his leadership in parish activities. Parish programs should aim not to entertain the members but to provide a contact point between the "inside" and the "outside" of the church. Sunday services, too, should outfit members with the "equipment of saints" (Eph. 4:12) so as to help them to carry out their apostolate in the world. The race crisis is a very serious matter, but pathological preoccupation with race problems will not bring us nearer to wholesome solutions. The race crisis is a symptom of a much deeper sickness in our society and in our churches and not the cause of the sickness.

Action and the Community at Large

The action of a pastor on race relations should be such that it enhances the building of communication between races, and also between groups of opposing viewpoints within a given race. Every pastor must, and I emphasize must, realize that his action *alone* will accomplish little. The problems created by the race crisis are much too big for an individual crusader to tackle alone. Even if we had thousands of such individuals, so long as they operate as "individual crusaders," their impact upon society will be negligible.

ACTION IN CONCERT WITH OTHERS.   The pastor must learn to work in concert with various organized groups in the community. In all his actions he ought to have the backing of his congregation. This is, of course, far less exciting than getting up on a Monday, going to Mississippi, being arrested, being bailed out, returning home on Saturday, and mounting the pulpit on Sunday as a hero. (Although in certain circumstances such a witness is certainly valid.) A pastor will usually be well advised to learn to work behind the scene, unnoticed by the public.

CREATING A WHOLESOME SOCIAL CLIMATE FOR SOUND RACE RELATIONS.   Social climate is crucially important to sound race relations. When race *per se* is allowed to become the focus of discussion, it is likely to divide the community into different camps, and communication between races deteriorates in no time. Where communication has already collapsed, pastors have a responsibility to enlarge perspectives to enable both sides to see the race problem in proper context and for what it really is. The example of Little Rock is instructive. There, the power structure of the city gradually united to move in the direction of desegregation of schools—but only after they faced other issues fundamental to the well-being of the city, from the standpoint of business and industry, as well as the future of their own children. What appeared at first to be undesirable, or at best barely tolerable, soon became a necessity.

In this connection we need to consider how mobile our population is and how interrelated all parts of the nation are to one another. We must educate our children to prepare them for such a mobile society. If they are to be useful citizens of tomorrow, they must be prepared to accept a multiracial society, no matter where they may live now, and no matter what vocations they may select. Our society cannot escape this responsibility. The sooner and the more thoroughly every school becomes racially integrated, the more firmly assured the happiness of the children attending it will be. Such a point of view will not become prevalent, however, until people begin to look at school desegregation in a wider perspective than that of race relations alone. To expedite the spread of such a point of view is one of the primary responsibilities of Christian pastors in every community today.

Let us consider, briefly, what action will be required of individual pastors to bring about a wholesome social climate, which is a necessary precondition for effective implementation of such objectives as open occupancy (or desegregation of residential areas), equal opportunity for employment (or fair employment practice), equal access to public accommodations, and, of course, desegregation of schools. Social climate is an expression of the collective will of the community. *With it* the community will be able to identify the problems and find ways and means to face them creatively and, finally, to solve them. *Without it* no demonstrations, direct actions, pressures, and the like subscribed to by dedicated people will achieve the desired end. Where there is not a positive social climate, and therefore no creative program, minority groups become impatient and resort to more drastic methods to make known their grievances and dissatisfactions. In most communities today the prevailing social climate with respect to race relations is essentially negative. What, then, should pastors do to improve the social climate in their communities?

The pastor's personal action as an isolated individual amounts to little. He must, in concert with others, act as a catalyst in community efforts to build communication among all sectors and segments of the poulation and to keep it flowing, in order that unfounded rumors and loose talk will not drive people into panic. This endeavor may well include urging the local power structure to establish an appropriate commission of multiracial composition, but it cannot stop with that. Legislative activities are another area where the pastor's influence may be constructively exercised.

The Pastor and His Professional Colleagues

It is important to stress the ecumenical character of the race crisis. Division of Christian people is a sin in that it is contrary to the will of God, whether the division is on the basis of doctrine, polity, race, ethnic, or class difference. Preoccupation with dogma, liturgical practice, or biblical interpretation in the interest of Christian unity is inexcusable if at the same time we ignore the painful reality of race separation within a confessional body. And such indifference to the realities of the race crisis makes a mockery of ecumenical enterprises. Furthermore, any system of theology that does not address itself seriously to the disunity of Christian people on a race basis is bad theology. For one Christian not to trust or be trusted by another Christian is a violation of Christian teaching. It makes, in fact, a mockery of Christian worship (Matt. 5:23 ff.).

Christian action in dealing with race relations must, therefore, be ecumenical—interconfessional and interracial —and local action must be an integral part of national and indeed world-wide action by the Church universal. A *genuine fellowship of pastors* transcending confessional and race differences, with express concern for the general welfare of the community at large, transcending immediate needs (however keenly felt) of respective congregations, will be a quick but effective "well-spring" of a positive social climate. Here, again, the key is "express concern for the general welfare of the community at large," which is one of the manifestations of the missionary (or apostolic) posture of the congregations represented by the pastors involved.

When such concern is vital, all sorts of ecumenical actions are possible: participating in various legislative activities; sponsoring an exchange of students between northern and southern colleges; exchanging memberships as domestic missionaries between parishes of different races on a limited basis. These and other actions conceived, formulated, and carried out ecumenically with full participation of congregations, after appropriate training, preparation, and discipline will help to generate a new and positive social climate in a community. This, in turn, will make it possible for a community to face the race crisis in relevant and creative ways.

Emphasis on the crucial importance of social climate must not be misconstrued to mean that the Church or the pastor should not act until a favorable climate is formulated. On the contrary, the Church must act to build that climate. It is often said, "We cannot legislate morality," which is true, but legislation establishes an institutional framework (and thereby a social climate) within which moral principles can be put into practice. Passage of civil rights legislation will not automatically eliminate race discrimination, but it is a decisive step toward it, in that it sets up unequivocal standards upon which judgments can be based. It is important that pastors lead their congregations in legislative activities where such are needed, so that the Christian community may help to build the social climate and the moral standards of our society. Far too often the Church has done no more than conform to establish mores, and has neglected its responsibility to assist in setting wholesome standards.

Do not say, "It won't work," until an attempt has been made to try out some constructive actions. If the current crisis is, as we have suggested, an indication of the serious social revolution our nation and the world are undergoing, then the churches must be prepared to undergo radical reformation themselves.

Christians of all denominations must join hands and together move forward, for they are, by the grace of God, the salt of the earth and the light of the world, chosen by our Lord to carry on his Mission in the world—to reconcile men to men, and reconcile them in one new body to God, and thus to fulfill the redemption of the world!

Christian Unity
and the Race Issue

IN recent years, the apostolate (or sentness) of the Church has been emphasized anew by theologians, especially in ecumenical circles. Professor Hendrik Kraemer, for one, has repeatedly said that it is not that the Church *has* a mission but that the Church *is* Mission. That is to say, the Church is the People of God, chosen by God out of many peoples, or nations, of the world, and sent into the world (as apostles) to participate in the ministry of his Son Jesus Christ, the ministry of redemption whereby to reconcile the world now estranged to God.

The Church Is *Mission*

Evidence of our estrangement from God is readily found in the divisions which beset us in many ways: the perversion of relationships between male and female, tensions between races, and conflicts between nations. Another manifestation is the conflict between social classes (the haves and the have-nots). These divisions should not be thought of as static states of alienation, but rather, in more dynamic terms, as divisive forces constantly at work within the social structure and within the human personality.

There is a sense in which Sin is a collective name for such divisive forces that tend to destroy the unity of mankind created in the beginning by God to live in harmony with one another, namely, in community.

The Church, then, finds itself in a world torn by the divisive forces of Sin, obligated to reconcile one to another peoples of the world now variously set against each other. It is the mission of the Church to restore the broken unity of mankind, and to bring the reunited world back to God. Since this is the vocation of the Church in the world, the interior division of the Church is intolerable. But the Church is divided, precisely because *it is in the world*. The forces which have divided the world have also divided the Church. The division of the Church is not solely a matter of difference in doctrinal position or theological conviction, but much more deeply ingrained in the very nature of man, redeemed once and for all by Christ though we are. Divisions of race within the Church need to be approached from this standpoint, not merely as moral issues. We cannot ignore the fact that when one group of Christians says to another group of Christians of the same persuasion (or the same ecclesiastical tradition), "We cannot worship God in Jesus Christ together," it is a profoundly theological statement. It is precisely theology that is challenged. To treat such attitudes as "nontheological" is to neglect profoundly the witness of theology.

No attempt will be made here to review the central doctrines of the Church, such as those of Creation and Redemption, of Man and his Fall, of the Church and the World. What is intended is to give close attention—analytical from the point of view of race and ethnic relations—to the historical and cultural context within which the contemporary churches must be *the* Church, One, Holy, Catholic, and Apostolic. Our subject matter, in other words, is theological, but the method of discussing it will be sociological. No attempt at a synthesis of theology and sociology is intended, however, but rather the start of some dialogue *between* theology and sociology. The reason for this is simple: Sound Christian theology must take God's creation seriously, and this requires, among other things, that theology look deeply at the world as it is—now, here, and full of sin.

Congregations Based upon Race or Ethnic Origin

Congregations organized according to race, ethnic origin, language difference, or other cultural considerations are increasing in number, and are an important phenomenon in our more and more open, pluralistic society.

Their existence is a reality, and will continue to be, and we are compelled to accept them as part of the context of the race crisis. In some cases the churches are segregated only at the local level, but in others whole denominations (or confessions) are composed of one race or other special constituency. We accept them as they are, and ask two interrelated questions about them.

1. Can such a church be *the* Church in the full sense of the term? Or, to put it differently, are individual members of any one of these churches partaking of the ministry of the Church in full?

2. Does the existence of such churches violate the unity of Christian people in Christ?

Manifestly, if the answer to the first question is negative, then the answer to the second is also negative.

According to the doctrine that where the Word is preached and the sacraments administered, there is the Church of Jesus Christ, there is no reason, in theory anyway, why there should not be a racially organized church. Considered from the standpoint of the congregation, the same doctrine may be restated to read: where the Word is *heard* and the sacraments are *received*. If this doctrine is to be meaningful we must add the words "with understanding" to both "heard" and "received." The moment the words "with understanding" are added, we are forced to recognize the positive argument for a racially organized local congregation. (A racially organized denomination poses a different problem.) The Word, if it is to be heard "with understanding," must be preached in a language the congregation understands—"language," that is, in the linguistic and in the cultural sense. It would seem almost mandatory, in certain circumstances, for an ethnic congregation to be established, for example, for immigrants. It certainly appears to meet the immediate need of a given group within the context of a given situation. But we must be relentless and ask, "Does it really?"

From the standpoint of those who adhere to the doctrine of a *territorial church* with parish and diocese as locally embodied units of a catholic Church, such an approach does more to create a problem than to solve it. From the standpoint of those who adhere to the doctrine of a *gathered church* with emphasis on the individual's response and commitment to the call, such an approach has much to recommend it, and even appears a natural development.

From an empirical (rather than a doctrinal) standpoint,

however, the question is whether the members of a racially organized congregation are actually receiving the full ministry of the Church. We may ask: Is *all* that makes *a* church *the* Church found in such a congregation? Is the presence of properly ordained ministers who preach the Word and administer the sacraments all that is necessary to make *the* Church of such a congregation?

These questions, in turn, lead us inescapably to ask another question: When a man or a woman participates in the life of such a congregation and, in particular, attends the Sunday service, how much of his or her person is there? When a West Indian migrant in London confines his "church life" to an exclusively West Indian congregation, much of his "real life" throughout the week will be left out of his church life. His church life may even become little more than an escape from real life. It may be comfortable (even comforting) to him to return on Sunday to his old country, its language, its culture, and its customs. He feels at home among his own people, sheltered from the cold reality of life in which he has to be constantly on his toes competing with "native" (British) people. But is this what the migrant really needs? Is it enough for the Church to provide him with a cultural and emotional shelter in a new and strange country? The migrant lives among and works with the "native" people, whether he has mastered their language or not. From the moment he lands in Britain, the West Indian begins to share in the life of the British people and he becomes a part of it. If he is to hear the living Word of God, he must hear it within this context and not outside it. The congregational life which is truly meaningful to him must be such that it embraces the whole of his life.

Similar situations confront Negro people in American cities, African people in Johannesburg, American people in Tokyo, and so on. Customarily, special congregations have been set up for such people, for reasons of language, race, culture, and the like. The assumption seems to have been that religion is a "personal" (or private) matter most effectively practiced entirely in private or in the company of congenial people. Such an argument falls far short of the basic criterion, "all in each place," which defines the unity of the Church. A racially organized congregation in a multiracial society is, therefore, untenable. It is no more tenable than would be a congregation made up exclusively of employers and their families, or exclusively of day laborers and their families. What would we say about a congregation (even multiracial) made up exclusively of Republicans or Democrats in the United States, or exclusively of Tories or Laborites in Great Britain? How about a congregation composed exclusively of men or of women? A local congregation must include in it people reflecting the total composition of the community in which it exists and to which it is intended to minister.

"That They May All Be One"

The doctrinal arguments in favor of racially or culturally "gathered" churches lead inevitably to *apartheid* in South Africa and residential segregation in the United States and other countries. It is difficult to see how such conditions can be justified unless *apartheid* or residential segregation results in two sovereign nations independent of each other, related to each other only through diplomatic exchange. Even sovereignty, however, can no longer keep people from sharing a common destiny nowadays. (This is exemplified in the development of the European Common Market, the British Commonwealth, the French Community, even in NATO, SEATO, and so forth. We are finding that geopolitical boundaries cannot keep one people completely apart from another.) Everybody is involved in, and related to, everybody else in a rapidly "shrinking" world.

It is to this basic solidarity of all mankind that the gospel addresses itself: "You have heard that they were told, 'You must love your neighbour and hate your enemy.' But I tell you, love your enemies and pray for your persecutors, so that you may show yourselves true sons of your Father in heaven, . . . So you are to be perfect, as your heavenly Father is" (Matt. 5:43-48).

The parable of the Good Samaritan likewise points to the basic oneness of all mankind transcending race, culture, and other differences (Luke 10:25-37; see also, Rom. 3:29; 10:12; 11:25, 32; Gal. 3:26-28; Col. 3:11; Eph. 1:10, 22; 2:11-22; 4:3-6). In Christ men's eyes are opened to the basic oneness of all mankind. An exclusive "fellowship" of Christians only is not compatible with the teaching of Christ or the message of the gospel.

We are challenged to think carefully about the unity of the Church in relation to the wholeness of locally or nationally (or even denominationally) organized bodies. Historically, there is a sense in which a certain geographical territory has been a local "unit" of the Church universal. The assumption seems to have been that there should be one church in one territory, and that this church was an integral part of the Church universal, just as the territory itself was an integral part of the world. Participation in the Church universal is basic if a local church is to be *the* Church; and a local church does not become qualified to

join the Church universal merely by fulfilling certain prescribed rules and regulations.

Every Church denomination now claims to be *the*
Church. Is this claim theologically tenable? If it is, what are
we to make of the multiplicity of the universal Church? If
it is not, how are we to achieve the unity of the Church
apart from (or short of) organic reunion of all churches?

To make the same point in a different way: Every man
(including every Christian) is the product of a particular
culture, a particular race, a particular nation, and a particular historical period. Manhood is thus "embodied" in him
in a peculiar and unique way, and his individuality is a con-
figuration of many particular factors. And every Christian
is, furthermore, of a particular tradition. Therefore, there
can no more be a pure and perfect Church than there can
be a pure and perfect man or a pure and perfect Christian.
It is bad theology not to take account of the social and historical limitations of all churches when trying to understand the basis of Christian unity. Every existing church
must, empirically, be accepted as an integral part of the universal Church. Thus we are compelled to accept ecclesiastical pluralism in every part of the world.

Is this problem limited to the transitional period in which
we find ourselves, and soon to be over? No. Successive (and
mounting) waves of immigration make it a recurrent, if not
a permanent, phenomenon. Inevitably this means we are
likely to have with us always churches that are composed
according to race or ethnic origin. At the same time, we
must recognize that the second and third generations of
immigrant communities participate increasingly in the
mainstream of their new society (in education, employment, recreation, social intercourse, and so on). Friendships

are formed, business partnerships develop, marriages take place between members of different churches. In this context "racial congregations" and "ethnic churches" begin to become superfluous.

What Is the Vocation of the Divided Churches?

Ecclesiastical relations today, like race relations in recent decades, are not easily defined, partly as a consequence of missionary activities. While theologians and ecclesiastics debate potential intercommunion, intermarriage is taking place among thousands of Christians (including a number of clergymen). In such a situation the question, What is the vocation of racially and ethnically organized congregations? is a serious and important one for the churches. There are no adequate theological criteria to guide us because, traditionally, theology has not seriously concerned itself with the division of the Church based on race and ethnic origin.

Professor Herbert G. Blumer, a social scientist, has noted that in dealing with race relations in the contemporary situation, no theory of "universals" is of much use, and therefore we must turn to "policy" theory, or "theory which is designed to analyze given concrete situations as a basis for the devising of policy and the guidance of actions." *

In this sense, what we need, it seems to me, is a theory which will deal with such questions as the following:

1. How should the Church minister to minorities in a

* Herbert G. Blumer, "Reflections on Theory of Race Relations," in Andrew Lind (ed.), *Race Relations in World Perspective* (Honolulu: University of Hawaii Press, 1955), p. 21.

pluralistic society, given their conflicting needs to be integrated in a difficult environment and to assert their dignity rooted in a traditional culture?

2. How can the Church minister to the children of such people, whose emotional needs are radically different from those of their parents?

If a church based upon race (or ethnic origin) answers the first question, it certainly does not answer the second. If a policy of integration answers the second, it probably does not answer the first. This raises a third question:

3. Should there be a "separated" ministry, at least as a transitional measure, organizing a racial congregation for one generation while integrating the next into a church more appropriate in the community? If so, what sort of relationship should there be between parents who belong to one congregation and children who belong to another, or for that matter, between the clergy of the two congregations? How can such a ministry be carried out in practice? What does it take to make it effective? How can the two be coordinated and, ultimately, "integrated"?

These questions lead inevitably to another:

4. Are there situations in a pluralistic society which make it necessary for a racial congregation or an ethnic church to be established permanently? Can a racial congregation or an ethnic church have "all in each place"? How can it be so established as to remain an integral part of the universal Church?

We must not close our eyes to situations where racial and ethnic churches have been perpetuated for no other reason than to conform to the pattern of race discrimination as practiced in a surrounding society. The question that arises out of this misfortune may be stated as follows:

5. What must be done with the racial or ethnic churches now in existence which have no reason to be perpetuated other than to conform and thus to give assent to race discrimination as practiced in a given society?

Churches have tended to avoid these questions by resorting to ideas of "congeniality" of the church, an institution supposed to be made up of people who share a language, or a culture, or a race, or some such thing. But this approach neglects two crucial questions: (1) Is the whole of the Church's ministry being received by the whole man in such a church; and (2) Is such a church really the local embodiment of the universal Church? The answer must be negative, because (1) such a church is only an artificial "island" in a pluralistic society, and fails to reflect the interrelationship of people with each other, and (2) confronted by race discrimination, the Church must emphasize the ministry of reconciliation between alienated races.

We must, furthermore, remember that even uniracial (one race) congregations become internally divided when race issues are acute. It is not only the chasm between races which grows wider, but members of one race divide on account of different attitudes toward the other race. In such situations the churches have not, for the most part, realized that what is involved is a denial of Christian unity. Why? Drawn into political issues, the churches have assumed that civil rights are less important than church unity. Concern for Christian unity ("all in each place") has become a force which undermines the unity of those already covenanted together in a congregation (or denomination).

Churches today desperately need a "policy" that confronts these and other related questions. Nothing is more urgent from the standpoint of effective pastoral ministry in the contemporary world. How can we develop such a policy? Can it be *deduced* from traditional doctrines of the Church? Can dogmatic or biblical theology help? Sound theology on these race problems will turn to the social sciences to make a contribution. To develop a policy with respect to contemporary race relations we must have "an intimate knowledge of the given concrete situation, its people, their traditional views, their present run of attention, and the forces at work among them." Furthermore, in the light of a concrete situation so analyzed we must "assess the possible consequences of various alternative schemes of action." *

In a racially divided world how can Christian unity be achieved? To this question, no categorical answers, however sound from a theological standpoint, are sufficient. It requires an honest debate on race issues between theologians and social scientists—not to discuss theological issues in the abstract, but to analyze and evaluate the total situation within which actions toward unity must be taken.

What is Christian unity short of reconciliation among racial and ethnic groups within the Church? How can the racial and ethnic groups be reconciled one to another which have for so long been alienated one from another, even within the Church? It cannot possibly be achieved without a clear discernment on the part of Christian people of what God has been and still is doing in and through the contemporary racial conflicts the world over.

* *Ibid.*

Epilogue

THE scope and the intensity of race tensions in the United States should lead us to re-examine, honestly and humbly, our concept of the ministry of the Church, not only to members of ethnic or race minorities but to all people. In this Epilogue I would like to share my thoughts on some of the key issues involved, in the hope that some contribution may be made to an adequate ministry. What I will say is based upon and is a conclusion from the arguments I have advanced in this book.

The Church's Ministry to the Whole World

I am firmly convinced that one basic, if not the only, reason the Church has so far been miserably ineffective in dealing with the race crisis, both within the Church and without, is that its professional leadership (the clergy) has utterly failed to comprehend the problem in its proper frame of reference. This has happened because the clergy have no clear idea of what the ministry of the Church is, or more to the point, of what the Church is. In 1945, during World War II, Dr. F. Ernest Johnson, in a critical review of behavioral patterns among American Protestants, especially clergy, pointed out that "the free-lance character of their pulpit performances accentuated the individualism of

American Protestantism." Let me quote from Dr. Johnson's words of the 1940's:

> By what right does a Protestant minister decide in his own study, even on his knees, that his church is to participate, or is not to participate, in the war? . . . If the church is a real spiritual community in which the minister is not a dictator but only "first among equals," what he does as leader of the congregation is not to be unilaterally decided. Prophecy is not mere proclamation, and the offering of public prayer is not a private office. Both should come from the heart of the religious community itself. The minister contributes his insights, fostered by the discipline of his vocation, and his gift of articulation. The soul that cries out is that of the Church.

> All this serves to highlight a conspicuous weakness in our churches—the lack of any clear understanding of what the church is as a corporate community.*

During the subsequent years race relations have reiterated the validity of Dr. Johnson's observations. Churches in the United States, especially Protestant churches, suffer now even more from the twin ills of individualism and clericalism, stemming from a lack of theological understanding of the corporate nature of the Church and its ministry. The locally organized congregation has become a club of like-minded people (those who think of Jesus in a more or less similar way), and its pastor a professional expert on religion in much the same way a doctor is on medicine, or a lawyer on law. Each member of the congregation is consigned the right to act and behave according to

* "What Has the War Taught the Churches?" in F. Ernest Johnson (ed.), *World Order: Its Intellectual and Cultural Foundations* (New York: Institute for Religious Studies, available through Harper & Row, 1945), p. 234.

the dictates of his own conscience, including the right to take or leave whatever "professional advice" his pastor may give him. Furthermore, the Church as an institution, whether a local congregation or a larger denominational unit, has taken on the characteristics of a business corporation (except, perhaps, for "profit-making"). The clergy has become a professional staff "executive" accountable to dues-paying members who function as "stockholders." No one says outright that the clergyman is a paid employee, and the vestry a board of directors, but the behavior of a majority of churches betrays how widespread and deep-seated this notion is. Upon such a premise, the pastor is certain to become an "organization man," whose preoccupation is "how to run *my* parish successfully and make it prosper," and he will inevitably resort to such status symbols as a new organ or a new educational plant. He cannot avoid becoming preoccupied with the *felt* needs of *his* flock, who are none other than *his* supporters, rather than their *real* needs as the people of God sent into this world to carry out God's ministry of reconciliation!

Most public worship, liturgical or otherwise, has become little more than "private devotion in public." We go to *our* church to worship God in company with *our* kind of people, leaving the world behind and especially those who are not *our* kind. Consequently, most services of Holy Communion are a mockery of corporate worship. In the Episcopal Church worshipers say in the prayer of post-Communion thanksgiving:

Almighty and everliving God, we most heartily thank thee, for that thou dost vouchsafe to feed us who have duly received these holy mysteries, with the spiritual food of the most precious Body and Blood of thy Son, our Saviour Jesus

Christ; and dost assure us thereby of thy favour and goodness towards us; and that we are very members incorporate in the mystical body of thy Son, which is the blessed company of *all faithful people;* and are also heirs through hope of thy everlasting kingdom, by the merits of his most precious death and passion. And we humbly beseech thee, O heavenly Father, so to assist us with thy grace, that we may continue *in that holy fellowship,* and *do all such good works as thou hast prepared for us to walk in;* through Jesus Christ our Lord, to whom, with thee and the Holy Ghost, be all honour and glory, world without end. Amen.*

The Episcopal liturgy is explicit that the service of Holy Communion is *the* sacrament of the Church *as a community* in which are incorporated "*all* faithful people," and that each individual Christian can fulfill his discipleship and apostleship only by being a vital and integral part or sharer "in that holy fellowship." Failing this, he cannot begin to "do all such good works as thou hast prepared for us to walk in." It is clear that race segregation not only inflicts human indignity upon the *segregated* (an inexcusably unchristian thing to do to anybody), but also and more seriously, it cuts the *segregator* from the wellspring of his Christian life, a life in grace.

The clergy, in whom the responsibility of professional leadership for the Church's ministry in the world has been placed, must therefore consider the ministry of *all* Christians as a body—a corporate entity involving all Christians throughout the world, through all ages, at once including and transcending all races, colors, nationalities, cultures, languages, social classes, and any other distinctions whatsoever. This is the meaning of what is commonly called

* The Book of Common Prayer (italics added).

"the ministry of the laity." And laity here means the People of God as a whole, including the clergy. It is in this context that we are compelled to rethink what the specific roles and functions (vocation) of the clergy are. If the clergy are not "specialists in religion," as physicians are in medicine, or lawyers in law, what is the professional competence which distinguishes them from laymen (nonprofessionals) in the Church? What is their responsibility toward laymen, individually and collectively? These questions are far from being answered today, and our honest confrontation of the race crisis compels us to ask them, however much we might prefer to "leave well enough alone."

"Christ Is All, and in All."

The clergy are called to minister to the people of God, on the one hand, and the people of the world, on the other. The former are "ambassadors of God" sent into the world to reconcile the latter, the "estranged from God," to God. In 1959 Professor Dan Dodson, addressing the Methodist Conference on Human Relations at Southern Methodist University, Dallas, Texas, said: "There is a growing preoccupation in both theology and the behavioral sciences with the phenomenon of 'alienation' as modern man searches for authenticity of selfhood in an increasingly segregated environment."

How far has this preoccupation become a central concern of the pastoral (and evangelical) ministry being pursued day in and day out, week in and week out, year in and year out, by the ordinary clergy of this country? What proportion of the clergy now active in pastoral ministry are involved enough in, and detached enough from, the phenomenon of self-estrangement to be able to deal with it *existentially?* Most clergymen are either too involved ("organization men") or too detached ("arrived," in the worldly sense, aloof from and indifferent to the agony of people who are struggling to find their identities). What are the "vocational disciplines" (to use Dr. Johnson's term) which equip the ordinary clergy for such a complicated task?

The race crisis forcefully discloses that self-estrangement in modern society is not so much a result as a basic cause of discrimination and segregation. Where has such self-estrangement come from? It has come from the nature, or rather the structure, of modern technical and industrial society.

Modern industry has created literally thousands of . . . new occupations, for which there exist no occupational names that have any social significance outside of the particular industry, factory, or even department, in many cases. As a consequence, the wages attaching to these jobs become the most important outer symbol of their social value to the community.*

Modern man is largely lost in the uncharted wilderness of his industrial and technological society, which is also increasingly an open and a mass society. Population mobility, vertically and horizontally, is taking place with bewildering rapidity. In this situation, it is not surprising that *unredeemed* man, inwardly fragmented, seeks self-identity in one or another available group—race, nation, class. Rac-

* Roethlisberger and Dickinson, *Management and the Worker* (Cambridge, Mass.: Harvard University Press, 1935); quoted by Robert S. Lind, "Groups and Social Status," in R. M. MacIver (ed.), *Civilization and Group Relations* (New York: Harper & Row for Institute for Religious Studies, 1945), p. 98.

ism, prevalent among civilized people, intelligent and well-to-do, is a vestige of tribalism, and for this reason is extremely difficult to overcome.

The Christian response to this need of modern man is that he should abandon his former identity based on race, clan, tribe, nation, or class, and accept a completely new identity in Christ. "From now on, therefore, we regard no one from a human point of view; . . . if any one is in Christ, he is a new creation; the old has passed away, behold, the new has come. All this is from God, who through Christ reconciled us to himself." (2 Cor. 5:16 ff.). "For you have died, and your life is hid with Christ in God. . . . Do not lie to one another, seeing that you have put off the old nature with its practices and have put on the new nature, which is being renewed in knowledge after the image of its creator. Here there cannot be Greek and Jew, circumcised and uncircumcised, barbarian, Scythian, slave, free man, but Christ is all, and in all" (Col. 3:3-11).

These passages are not moral injunctions, but descriptions of fact, of an existing state of affairs for each man who in Christ has been reconciled to God. A new man, who has "put on Christ" (Rom. 13:14) has, furthermore, been incorporated into his body, the Church. "For as many of you as were baptized into Christ have put on Christ. There is neither Jew nor Greek, there is neither slave nor free, there is neither male nor female; for you are all one in Christ Jesus" (Gal. 3:27 f.).

St. Paul does not say, notice, that he who professes himself a Christian must disregard his own race, or social status, or even sexual difference, or such differences in others, but, knowing who he really is, he does not any longer need to take refuge in such partial identities. Once a man is incorporated into the Church, the community of all faithful people, then race, color, social status, and even sex, become irrelevant. The man has become a *person* in Christ.

Developing Sound Pastoral Theology

What has gone wrong and where, that many apparently devout Christians are also racists, and many Christian congregations are bulwarks of race segregation in the United States? The answer is that organized churches in this country have not often been *the* Church but something less or other than *the* Church, and the Christian ministry has not dared or cared to confront the apostasy of the churches. How can we expect a local congregation to become racially inclusive when it has been permitted to exist and prosper primarily if not solely as a symbol of social status or something comparably irrelevant! Attempts to desegregate such a congregation for the sake of desegregation alone will quite understandably meet only stubborn resistance. Attempts to persuade such a congregation on grounds of decisions of the Supreme Court or Civil Rights laws disregard the basic problem: the apostasy of the church, and the adulteration of Christian ministry. In many ways organized Christianity in the United States has been everything but *the* Church. In race relations, it has acted as though it were a civil rights organization, a community agency, an educational or philanthropic institution, or a society of "do-gooders," but seldom has it acted as *the* Church.

How can this failure be corrected? Before anything else, the professional leadership of the church must be educated, trained, and disciplined to consider race problems primarily in the context of pastoral theology rather than social ethics. The race crisis is, of course, a matter of personal morality and social justice, but it is also much more. It is a profound sickness in our society or culture with which most people are afflicted, personally and collectively. To minister to men living under the burden of such a complex sickness, the professional leadership of the Church desperately needs the complete discipline of pastoral theology.

What is necessary is a discipline that defines theologically the meaning of identity in Christ within the culture and in the concrete situation which exists *here* and *now*. What more is required of a Christian than that he regularly attend church services and financially support the institutions of the church? To answer this simple question realistically demands the exercise of many disciplines and vocations: biblical, historical, and systematic theology; the social and behavioral sciences (including depth-psychology and anthropology); philosophy; and history. What I have called pastoral theology, therefore, is a theological discipline providing a framework and a methodology such that experts in the various specialized disciplines are encouraged to converse, to collaborate, and to coordinate one with another.

It might seem to expect too much of local clergy to take part in the development of such a discipline, but it is they who need it most desperately. No matter how difficult it is, they must do so, because such a dynamic discipline cannot be developed by theologians or philosophers in some ivory tower or academic institution. We may hope (without much confidence) that theological seminaries will provide some theological foundation upon which pastors may build the necessary discipline. But the pastors themselves will have to engage experts in the specialized disciplines in vital conversation. If they do so with self-confidence and humility, conviction and open-mindedness, eventually we may arrive at a workable principle or theory of pastoral ministry.

Let there be no mistake. I do not say that bits and pieces of sociology, anthropology, psychology, psychiatry, and so on, added to biblical and systematic theology will accomplish anything. The pastor must not be an academic "jack of all trades," or an amateur psychotherapist, or amateur social scientist. He must, however, free himself of narrowly defined theological positions, and learn to relate his special knowledge to the knowledge of specialists in other disciplines. The pastor must, in other words, be a "new man in Christ," and as he relates himself to other people, he must consider them to be (at least potentially) new men in Christ. Pastoral theology has not so far taken account of this dimension, and it is urgent that the neglect be remedied.

The Answer Is the Cross

Let me say, in conclusion, that the approach I plead for in the current race crisis, would avoid judgment, on the one hand, and embrace crucifixion, on the other hand. People suffering from race prejudice would not be condoned or condemned. They would be invited to acknowledge their prejudice as sin against God himself, in order that forgiveness might come from God and from those whom they have wronged. This is, I believe, the meaning of reconciliation. People who have been the victims of prejudice would be invited to forgive the prejudiced and the history of prejudice which has been their suffering.

The pastor who ministers in this way to both sides will find himself suspect of both. He will not even have the consolation of being involved in a dramatic event. He will be lonely. Yet his ministry (merely a vehicle of divine forgiveness) will help to reconcile two opposing parties to one another and will help to create one new man from two. This is, I believe, the meaning of crucifixion. Crucifixion is no mere fiction, but stark reality, in this life, and apart from it reconciliation is wholly inconceivable. The way of the Cross is the only way to a vital community, and a vital community alone can reflect the witness of the Church in a divided world.

Suggested Reading List

AHMAN, Matthew, ed. *Race: Challenge to Religion* (Chicago: Henry Regnery Co., 1963). 178 pp.

CAMPBELL, Will D. *Race and the Renewal of the Church* (Philadelphia: The Westminster Press, 1962). 90 pp.

HASELDEN, Kyle. *The Racial Problem in Christian Perspective* (New York: Harper & Row, 1959). 222 pp.

KITAGAWA, Daisuke. *Race Relations and Christian Mission* (New York: Friendship Press, 1964). 190 pp.

LINCOLN, C. Eric. *The Black Muslims in America* (Boston: Beacon Press, 1961). 276 pp.

POPE, Liston. *The Kingdom beyond Caste* (New York: Friendship Press, 1957). 170 pp.

SILBERMAN, Charles E. *Crisis in Black and White* (New York: Random House, 1964). 370 pp.

TANNENBAUM, Frank. *Slave and Citizen: The Negro in the Americas* (New York: Random House—Vintage Books, 1963). 128 pp.

UNESCO. *The Race Question in Modern Science* (A Symposium) (Paris: UNESCO, 1956). 373 pp.

WOODWARD, C. Vann. *The Strange Career of Jim Crow* (New York: Oxford University Press—Galaxy Books, 1957). 183 pp.